$15.50

615.8515
R659T   95215
       DATE DUE

THERAPEUTIC RE-CREATION

Ideas and Experiences

By

FRANK M. ROBINSON, JR.

Associate Professor
Department of Recreation Education
Boston-Bouvé College
Northeastern University
Boston, Massachusetts

With a Foreword by
Catherine L. Allen
Dean
Boston-Bouvé College
Northeastern University
Boston, Massachusetts

CHARLES C THOMAS · PUBLISHER
Springfield · Illinois · U.S.A.

Published and Distributed Throughout the World by
CHARLES C THOMAS • PUBLISHER
Bannerstone House
301-327 East Lawrence Avenue, Springfield, Illinois, U.S.A.

This book is protected by copyright. No part of it may be reproduced in any manner without written permission from the publisher.

© *1974, by* CHARLES C THOMAS • PUBLISHER
ISBN 0-398-03160-6 (cloth)
ISBN 0-398-03161-4 (paper)
Library of Congress Catalog Card Number: 74-2181

With THOMAS BOOKS careful attention is given to all details of manufacturing and design. It is the Publisher's desire to present books that are satisfactory as to their physical qualities and artistic possibilities and appropriate for their particular use. THOMAS BOOKS will be true to those laws of quality that assure a good name and good will.

Printed in the United States of America
A-1

Library of Congress Cataloging in Publication Data

Robinson, Frank Melvin, 1928-
   Therapeutic re-creation.

   1. Recreational therapy. I. Title.
[DNLM: 1. Handicapped. 2. Recreation. 3. Rehabilitation. QT250 R659t 1974]
RM737.R6   615'.8515   74-2181
ISBN 0-398-03160-6
ISBN 0-398-03161-4 (pbk.)

FOREWORD

> There is one thing stronger than all the armies in the world: and that is an idea whose time has come.
>
> VICTOR HUGO

YOUNG GRADUATE STUDENTS with fresh unique ideas of theory and practice share with the reader their on-the-job daily experiences as therapeutic recreation educators in settings where the human spirit is at the core, at the heart of the program. The cruelly burned and disfigured child, the veteran with no legs, the retarded or severely disabled young adult, the emotionally disturbed boy, the prisoner, the old and deeply discouraged woman, . . .

In every human being there is an infinite need for personal expression, for creative experience, for aesthetic appreciation, for individual self-enhancement, for the respect and affection of one's fellows.

The climate for learning and dreaming and doing may be as diverse as the open field, the living room in the nursing home, the play center, the city street. Personal fulfillment, whatever the environment, is achieved with the realization that life has significance, and purpose, and meaning.

Philosophically, RE-creation of the body, mind and spirit is based in Man's three-fold nature—

> Man as an entity, a human being content to be alone to read, to pray, to craft, to listen to music, to study the stars. . . .
>
> Man as a social creature, a participant with the members of the church or temple or school or club, a bridge partner, a community worker, a vote getter. . . .
>
> Man as an integral part of God's Universe, alone or together to walk beside quiet streams, to plant flowers, to climb mountains, to be fully aware of the birds, the insects, the trees and the rocks, to breathe the freshness of sea air as the breakers roll in. . . .

It was ever so. When Man treasures time IN his hands rather than carries the heavy burden of time ON his hands, living is rich and full.

CATHERINE L. ALLEN

INTRODUCTION

Expanding leisure time in America has greatly influenced our way of life. We have noticed its spiralling effects on the economy as people seek to satisfy the urge to play and recreate. The *U.S. News and World Report*[1] states that 105 billion dollars was spent on various forms of active recreation opportunities, sports equipment, tourism, entertainment and other leisure interests in 1972. To provide expanded recreation services students are being professionally educated to plan and administer them. The Department of Labor[2] forecasts a bright job outlook for recreation in this 1970-80 decade by listing recreation as the second fastest growing occupation in the country. While such observations substantiate the tremendous impact of leisure on our culture and reveal its strong economic influence, it does not acknowledge the large segment of our population who are unable to purchase recreation or to participate in typical kinds of experiences or activities. These are the people with an over-abundance of leisure while frequently lacking sufficient resources to cope with it. They are found in treatment and rehabilitation centers, hospitals and extended care facilities; they are confined to wheelchairs, a prison cell or live a sheltered and disadvantaged existence in the community. For lack of an accurate all-inclusive term these people are referred to as "handicapped." It is to this group that our anthology is devoted.

The selections appearing in this book were written by young graduate students pursuing a master's degree in recreation. Most of them are employed as full-time recreation therapists while attending classes during the evening. Although the majority of students are relatively new to the field they speak from personal experience and welcome the opportunity to contribute to the paucity of literature in this developing area. Each author has

---

1. *U. S. News and World Report,* April 17, 1972, pp. 42-45.
2. *Changing Times, The Kiplinger Magazine,* June 1972, p. 9.

something original to say, which in itself is refreshing, and each has endured the hard labors of saying it in writing.

Re-creation is utilized in our title to give emphasis to the intended meaning of a word which is still, too often, misunderstood, mispronounced, downgraded or associated with only diversion or amusement. The first section is divided into major headings: the physically disabled, mentally retarded, emotionally and socially maladjusted and the elderly. This is followed by sections presenting various approaches and concerns for the therapist, leader, activity director, teacher and the general public. It is our primary purpose to relate new experiences, ideas and research that will be of value to the reader and help to bridge the knowledge gap in this exciting field.

>   RE-CREATE—It's right for man to create and it's also right for man to try again and again to create those experiences which bring fulfillment.

THERAPEUTIC RE-CREATION

ACKNOWLEDGMENTS

My grateful thanks to the graduate student authors of class 63.854 who have enthusiastically shared their experiences and ideas in the compilation of this manuscript.

I especially appreciate the direction and encouragement provided by Bob Parker of the English Department at Northeastern University and to Dr. Al McCay, Recreation Department chairman and Dean Allen for their support throughout.

The proofreading and editorial work has been scrutinized by Ruth Fabyan, my devoted mother-in-law, and our friend Marjorie Bruce. Their contributions have been immense.

CONTENTS

Page

Foreword—*Catherine L. Allen* v
Introduction vii
Acknowledgments ix

Section I
THE PHYSICALLY DISABLED

Chapter

1. THERAPEUTIC RECREATION AND THE BURNED CHILD
   Jacalyn Hamada 5
2. A PROGRAM FOR CHILDREN IN AN ACUTE HOSPITAL
   Joyce Koczan 21
3. CASE STUDY OF A DISABLED VETERAN
   Michael Sorter 30

Section II
THE MENTALLY RETARDED

4. HOGAN REGIONAL CENTER: A SCHOOL FOR THE RETARDED
   Christine Konieczny 37
5. DAY CAMPING FOR THE RETARDED
   Earl E. Vermillion and Charles L. Alongi, Jr. 45

Section III
THE EMOTIONALLY AND SOCIALLY MALADJUSTED

6. TAILORING RECREATION TO THE INDIVIDUAL IN A STATE PSYCHIATRIC HOSPITAL
   Stephen M. Killourhy 55
7. DOING TIME—THE PRISON SCENE
   Frank M. Robinson, Jr. 62

Section IV
THE ELDERLY

8. THE ROLE OF THE RECREATION THERAPIST IN THE LONG-TERM HEALTH CARE FACILITY
   Elizabeth C. Allen 79

Chapter   Page

9. STARTING A RECREATION PROGRAM WITH LIMITED FUNDING IN NURSING HOMES
   Linda Tracy Dudish 87

Section V

APPROACHES IN THERAPEUTIC RECREATION

10. INVESTIGATING MUSIC IN A THERAPEUTIC CAPACITY
    Christine A. Meda 101
11. WHAT CAN I BE? MUST I BE ME?
    Jacalyn Hamada 109
12. VOLUNTEER WORKREATION: A UNIQUE THERAPEUTIC MODEL
    Gwen Gutter 115
13. DEVELOPING A VOLUNTEER PROGRAM IN THE THERAPEUTIC SETTING
    Elise O'Brien 123

Section VI

CONCERNS IN THERAPEUTIC RECREATION

14. UNDERSTANDING THE USE OF PHARMACEUTICALS
    Wes Arens 137
15. IDENTITY PROBLEMS IN A HOSPITAL SETTING
    Susan Mattes 143
16. TRENDS IN MUNICIPAL RECREATION SERVICES FOR HANDICAPPED PEOPLE
    Debra S. Bloom 147
17. ATTITUDINAL BARRIERS
    Dwight Woodworth, Jr. 157
18. ARCHITECTURAL BARRIERS
    Nancy K. Williams 164
19. TOWARD INTEGRATION
    Frank M. Robinson, Jr. 173

THERAPEUTIC RE-CREATION

SECTION I
THE PHYSICALLY DISABLED

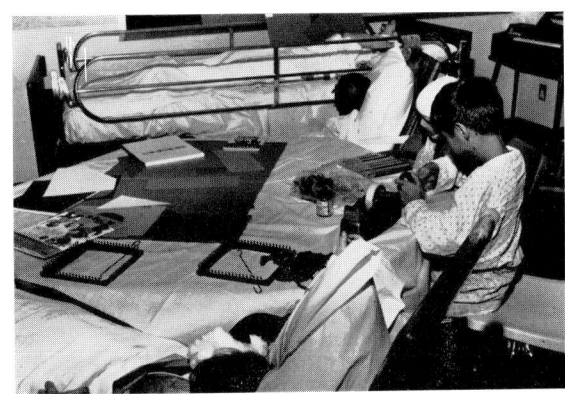

Courtesy of Shriner's Burn Institute Boston Unit

Courtesy of St. Vincent Hospital Worcester, Massachusetts

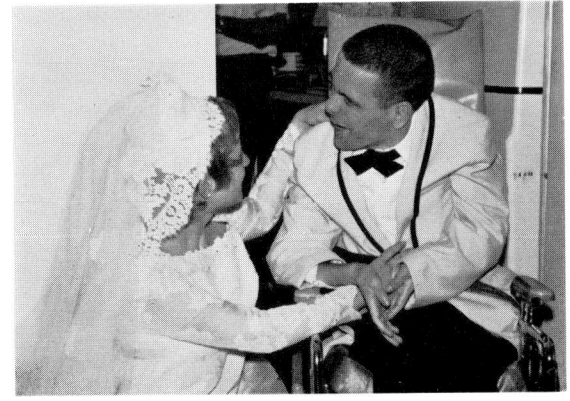

Jackie Kirkman—an inspiration to all who have known him

CHAPTER 1

THERAPEUTIC RECREATION AND THE BURNED CHILD

JACALYN HAMADA

Introduction

BOTH THE MENTAL and physical handicaps resulting from a severe burn are often overlooked in the textbook classifications of the disabled. A wealth of information is available on the medical aspects of the burn—the wound itself, its treatment, and its prognosis—but little has been written on the burn victim. In this paper, I shall attempt to present the basic recreation that supplements and complements the rehabilitation of the burn victim.

Burns are not selective. They can strike anyone, at any age, in any walk of life. Due to the broadness of this topic, I shall focus on the burned child—toddler to teenager—during his admission and subsequent reconstructive admissions. Viewing the possibilities of therapeutic recreation in the hospital, one can expand this program into an outpatient program in the home and community.

Definition

The American Heritage Dictionary of the English Language defines *burn* as a noun:

> An injury produced by fire, heat, or a heat producing agent. Burns are classified in order of increasing seriousness: a *first-degree burn* produces redness of the skin, a *second-degree burn* produces blistering, and a *third-degree burn* destroys and chars the skin tissue.[1]

Today, medical science has reevaluated the classifications of burns as follows: *first-degree burns* involve only the epidermis

---

1. *The American Heritage Dictionary of the English Language.* Boston, Houghton-Mifflin Company, 1970, p. 178.

and heal rapidly. Superficial *second-degree burns* involve the upper portion of the corium and many islets remain which proliferate to cover the area in about fourteen days. Deep *second-degree burns* extend into the corium, and the only epithelium remaining is the lining of the sweat glands and hair follicles. *Third-degree burns* involve the full thickness of skin and extend down to subcutaneous fat.[2] *Fourth-degree burns* destroy totally the living tissue and result in amputation.

Degree of Burn	Frequent Causes	Usual Appearance[3]	Healing Time[4]
1st	Sunburn, low intensity flame	Reddened	2-3 days
2nd	Liquids, scalds, flash fires	Mottled red areas, blistered, serous drainage, edema	5-15 days
3rd	Open fires, electricity	Charred, black or white, edema	Weeks
4th	Long exposure to flame, electricity	Gray, black	0

Who Gets Burned? And Why

The extent of burns is unknown. Minor burns are often treated without professional care. Major burns may be treated without the facts reaching the statistician. The facts and figures listed below are well-documented estimates. The actual extent of disability to the burn victim often depends on the amount of body area burned. Twenty years ago a 30 percent burn injury would usually have been fatal. Today burn saves are as great as 85 percent of the body area burned. Intermittent complications of sepsis, malnutrition, and respiratory complications are now the causes of a majority of burn fatalities.

Thirteen thousand children die yearly in the United States as a result of burn wounds or their complications.[5] From flammable fabrics alone there are an estimated 3,000 to 5,000 deaths and 150,000 to 250,000 injuries annually (adults and children).[6]

Any method of producing heat may result in a burn. The burn

---

2. Francine Margolius, "Burned children, infection, and nursing care," *Nurs Clin North Am,* 5 (1) :133.

3. *Ibid.*

4. John F. Burke, Modern burn therapy, *Sandoz Panorama,* November-December 1969, p. 5.

5. Margolius, *op. cit.,* p. 142.

6. *Flammable Fabrics,* Third Annual Report to the President. 1971, p. 3.

categories are flame, thermal, chemical, and electrical. (Respiratory burns are sometimes classified separately.) The age of a child plays an important role in the type of injury he sustains. These can be classified into four basic situations.

1. **INFANTS (6 MONTHS-1 YEAR).** The most common thermal injury in this age group occurs when a crawling infant sucks the free end of a "live" electric cord or may actually bite through an electrical wire. This results in deep facial burns involving the lips, tongue and other oral structures.
2. **TODDLER (2-4 YEARS).** A toddler often sustains a scald burn on his scalp, face, neck, shoulders, chest, and arms from tipping over a pan or pot containing a hot liquid on a stove.
3. **PRESCHOOL (4-8 YEARS).** A major portion of burns in this age group results from playing with matches.
4. **PREADOLESCENCE (8-12 YEARS).** Boys of this age group often sustain severe burns from gasoline or chemical explosions as a result of "experimenting." In addition, these boys often receive electrical burns as a result of tree climbing near power lines.
5. **YOUNG TEEN-AGERS (13-16 YEARS).** A young teen-age girl learning to cook, often receives severe burns reaching over open flames on a kitchen stove.[7]

One of the highest causes of severe burns is the flammable fabric. These fabrics may be ignited by anything from intense heat to electric sparks. As cited in *The Third Annual Report on Flammable Fabrics,* often the listed cause of a burn such as a match does not do the severe damage; it is the clothing which the match ignites that causes the greatest damage.

Sociological Profile

The following remarks lack statistical research and proof and should be so recognized. They do, however, represent my personal observations on the job in a close relationship to child and

---

7. Margolius, *op cit.,* p. 132.

parent. From what I have seen the young male from a broken lower-income home is the most likely candidate for a burn. It is common for burned children to come from homes with familial difficulty. The parents do not get along or are alcoholics or drug-users, the parents are separated or divorced, there have been several remarriages, or each child is by a different father (some fathers are unknown). Needless to say, family visits are confusing to the staff and often a cause of anxiety to the patient.

The burned child may also be the victim of child abuse. The parents' story may give it away, sometimes the doctor's examination may reveal the abuse, and sometimes it goes unnoticed. Many of the burn victims are so-called problem children; others may suffer minimal brain damage.

With complete disregard for the sociological profile, children from wealthy, educated, or "normal" backgrounds get burned too. Some accidents are avoidable, some are freak, but the child is the victim.

Sociological Impact of the Disability

The rare exception is that a burn does not leave a visible scar, deformity, or disability. The area of the burn has a tremendous effect on the force of the impact upon the individual and his relationships with others. Perhaps a sample case history will provide a small insight into the multiple problems in store for the burn victim, his family and community.

Jane is a five-year-old who wakes up one cold morning and decides to make herself some hot cereal. She pulls a chair up to the stove and begins to boil water. Her nightgown touches the flame and ignites. She cries for help. It takes Mommy and Daddy a few minutes, precious minutes, to awaken, realize what is going on, run downstairs, catch Jane who is now running in panic and extinguish the flames. She is rushed to the local hospital where initial treatment is administered. Without proper facilities for long-term care, the local hospital refers the patient to a burn hospital. Jane is admitted to the hospital, assessed as a 55 percent burn to chest, back, neck, arms, and parts of the face, and is placed in a BCNU.* Jane is semiconscious for the first few days;

---

* BCNU (Bacteria Control Nursing Unit), a plastic walled isolation unit with an air-flow device. The unit serves to reduce the possibility of cross-infection.

she feels relatively little pain since her burn is mostly third degree and has destroyed the nerve endings. During this time, Mommy and Daddy suffer from anxiety and guilt feelings. The inevitable "if only's" come to mind. Mommy blames Daddy for closing their bedroom door the night before (maybe Jane would have come to them for the cereal); Daddy blames Mommy, feeling she panicked, did not react quickly enough, and extinguished the flames incorrectly. Burns are ugly, it takes all their courage to see poor little Jane with tubes feeding her and wires suspending her; she's hurt so badly and she looks so little in that big bed. "My God, what will she look like? . . . Doctor, what are her chances? . . . Maybe she would be better off. . . . My God, what am I saying?" Jane stays in that unit for three months. Mommy and Daddy want to stay with her but there are three other sisters and brothers at home in Vermont. . . . What will become of them? Mommy and Daddy will visit on the weekends. Children, at this stage, are very astute and manipulative. The child will play the doctors and the nurses against one another and Mommy and Daddy against each other and the staff. The initial crisis has passed and Jane will make it. She will undergo many procedures of excision and grafting. The scars become more apparent. "Will those ugly scars ever go away? . . . Will she ever have breasts? . . . Will she ever know love and the touch of a man or will she repulse those who come near?" The family situation in Vermont has been regulated and has resumed a pseudo-normal pattern. Jane is at last ready to go home. She has large hypertrophic scars. Her neck, axilla, and hands are severely contracted, but her wounds have healed. She has many years of reconstructive surgery ahead of her, but the doctors feel it best that she have a rest from surgical procedures. The anxieties build up in the parents again. "How will the family react? . . . What will the other children say? . . . What will the neighbors think? . . . Will her little friends accept her? . . . Will she ever go to school?" Even Jane has expressed some query, but she is still young and resilient. Her time for doubt and anxiety is still ahead.

There are no easy solutions to the foreseeable problems. Life will never be the same for Jane's family. Strangers will stare and be quite rude and cruel with their questions. "Don't they realize that she is standing right here and can think and hear and feel?" Family support is a main factor in the emotional stabilization and adjustment of the burned child. Unfortunately, it is not the general rule. Some parents do not even want their children after a burn; schools do not want to accept responsibility; and uninformed parents feel their children will catch something by associating with children such as Jane. Successful adjustment can be attained, but it is a great deal of work requiring cooperation between parents, school, family and community.

The burn victim's initial hospital stay and further procedures (including home care) are very expensive. The average initial admission could run well over $8,000. Not all families are so lucky as to have these resources available. Often procedures must stop after completing absolute necessities for function, and cosmetic reconstructions such as the removal of visible scars must be foregone. This might cause the child some complicated emotional adjustments. Facial and hand scarring are usually the hardest adjustment. Colored stockings, long pants, and long sleeves may alleviate some initial social problems. The financial burden alone has a severe effect on the family life. Children may have to give up camp so Jane may have a necessary medical treatment; she does receive special attention and this is not always the prescription for family harmony.

The problems of adjustment exceed the time and space available to deal with them. Simply let the imagination run wild with complications, and maybe three-fourths of the subject may be covered.

Prognosis and Rehabilitation

The severely burned child faces from many weeks to many months of procedures on his acute admission. The usual routine for treatment begins with an initial evaluation and debridement of the child upon admission. Upon assessing the severity of the burn, the child is either placed in a BCNU, isolation room, or on the ward. Barring respiratory and smoke-inhalation damage or complications, an extensive burn usually requires primary excision (the removal of dead tissue) in order to facilitate healing.

The Burned Child

Then, healthy skin is cropped for grafting procedures; some may be applied at that time to the open areas; the remainder would be preserved for further procedures. If the child does not have enough healthy skin, the wound may be temporarily treated with allographs (skin from others with close tissue-type matches or cadavers), zenographs (pigskin), or an open treatment method. The open treatment method may be used if the wound is not too deep, but this method may cause severe contractures. The final grafting procedures are autographs (skin from one's own body). During these procedures body positioning and immobility is a key factor. Dressing changes occur often and are very painful. Splints and traction are often devised to prevent contractures and other possible disabilities which might arise out of a long-term stay in bed in one position. The continual fight is against bacteria which inhibits the healing of wounds, often doubling or tripling the healing time. Another battle is against malnutrition. The body often starves itself because the production of new skin requires an enormous amount of protein and calories.

Once the wounds have healed, there are many months and years of procedures ahead. Burn wounds often contract as a matter of course or because grafted skin may not always grow with the body. These contractures require surgical releases and physical therapy. Hypertrophic scars can be removed. Noses and lips can be rebuilt. Girls who have had third-degree chest burns can sometimes have breasts built and boys who have had their genitals damaged can sometimes have functioning or cosmetic organs rebuilt. Each goal requires many procedures and many months inside a hospital. Physical therapy plays a large role in the rehabilitative process. Outpatient visits to clinics and therapists continue for many months after discharge from the hospital.

Grafted skin may suffer from lack of sensation and discoloration. Usually the nerve endings grow with time and sensation begins again. Sometimes the discoloration disappears but the noticeable difference in skin color usually remains. Some of the difference can be covered cosmetically with make-up. Grafted skin is also sensitive to direct sunlight. Screens should be used and discretion applied in the planning of activities.

Recreational Therapy in the Hospital Setting: The Playroom Concept

The recreation therapist or "playlady," as she is commonly known in the hospital, should be a "safe" person. The word "safe" refers to the concept that nothing painful or unpleasant to the patient may be done in her presence. Hospital procedures always come first; at the necessary moment she will leave the child, explaining why she is leaving, in order to assure the constancy of the playlady-patient relationship. One can never force a child to play, but that is hardly necessary because play is probably the only contact that the child has with his life as it was before the admission. The playlady should attempt to contact all "her" children at least once a day. It is not always possible to spend time with each child but the constancy is necessary because the family does not always maintain a supportive relationship with the child. When the child begins to feel better, small projects in the form of arts and crafts or games enable him to feel that he can master something and often spark an improvement in morale. Remember, the child is forced to do many things he does not like to do during the course of a routine hospital day; he should not be forced to play or perform for the recreation therapist as well. The patient must feel that he is the master of his fate in at least one area.

The playroom concept should be an extension of the philosophy of the playlady. Again, there should be no medical procedures in the playroom. It is a "safe" area. The children should be free to come and go as they please, but the playlady and staff should encourage the child to visit the playroom as much as possible. This allows the child to escape the noise of the ward (dressing changes and procedures are very painful and therefore evoke screams and cries) and expend some of the restless energy that builds up in a restricted child. This relieves some of the disciplinary problems on the ward and also allows the nurses and housekeeping staff to take care of their duties without ambulating children underfoot. The playroom should be semi-structured and adaptable to the children's needs. Perhaps a project or two may be planned but most games and craft supplies should be available upon request. The playroom should be well equipped for all ages. Files should be kept so that at a moment's notice, the playlady may devise a program for a toddler or a teenager. Parents and visitors are welcome, but nonpatients should be watched. Often adults can speak without thinking and be as cruel as the uninformed "man on the street." While free play is a norm, utmost safety precautions should be maintained and normal courtesy should prevail.

Imagination and creativity will go a long way; kindness, attention, and affection will complete the job.

The Recreation Therapist as Part of the Team

The recreation therapist should be an integral part of the hospital team. She should work closely with the doctor, nurse, physical therapist, social worker and psychiatrist. The child is with the recreation therapist for a majority of his waking hours. If this time is used wisely, multifold results may occur. The following are a few examples of how a team effort works.

A child prone in bed for a long period may develop respiratory complications. There are standard exercises and devices for alleviating these conditions. Several children were either too young to use the device or too stubborn to participate in the exercises. The problem was brought to the playlady who in turn created activities (such as playing out the story of *The Three Little Pigs*) or found play items (such as balloons and pinwheels) to remedy the problem.

The healing of new skin requires large amounts of protein and calories. During the acute admission of a child, forced feeding is often necessary. The recreation therapist should not partake of these forced feedings because of their unpleasant naure. Medical science has devised a high protein drink which the children must consume several times a day; this is usually under great duress because even flavored "frappes," as they are called, taste terrible. Being a "safe" area, frappes are not permitted in the playroom, and the playlady will not approach a child with a frappe. However, the children know they cannot come into the playroom or cannot be visited by the playlady until they have finished their frappe, so they do. In the playroom, snacks are served, and during reconstructive procedures, the children may even make candy or cookies and the playlady will take the mixture to the kitchen for baking. The incentive to play frequently achieves medicinal ends.

Often the burned child will refuse to exercise fingers, arms or legs for the physical therapist. It is painful. With the knowledge of what needs to be exercised, the recreation therapist may devise games or crafts using the area in question. Bobby was a five-year-old who refused to walk on his burned foot. It had healed but he refused to put weight on it. After a twenty-minute tantrum, the physical therapist decided to try again later. Bobby was then brought into the playroom where there was a small horse on wheels. It was offered to him and placed a few steps away from him. No one would put him on it. After about ten minutes of eyeing the horse, he used a table for support and made it to the toy on his own. He then proceeded to walk-ride the horse for the morning. A tricycle has often done the same trick. The same is true with hand and finger exercise. Arts and crafts or changing a doll's clothes usually work for a girl and small sports games and motor car models for a boy.

Often a child will refuse to talk with a psychiatrist. This is true for several reasons: the hospitalized child is wary of doctors and can spot them in a minute; the child may be reluctant to talk with strangers about what is bothering him; the child may have been prejudiced against "shrinks—they're for crazy people." Close observation in the playroom and accurate reporting to the staff psychiatrist may help solve pent-up or budding emotional problems. Children will often play out their problems with other children or puppets which are always available in the playroom. Since the playlady is a "safe" person, the child may also confide in her for lack of anyone else who does not present a threat. The recreation therapist should always be aware of statements and questions, which may need pursuing, provided the situation is conducive to discussing the issue. Often this same confiding and playing out will reveal familial problems, child abuse and battering. These problems should be taken to the social worker. Foster homes may be necessary for certain children. Parents should be observed with their children. They may need counseling to help them deal with their child and the disability.

The group effort by the hospital team definitely makes for a more successful rehabilitative process.

Bacteria Control and Safety

The main fight in the burn hospital against bacteria must be waged in every corner of the hospital. Sepsis is the major killer of burn patients. Once a child is given a toy in BCNU, it does not come out until the child leaves the unit. This may mean months, so the therapist should try to plan expendable projects during this course of the admission. Strict antiseptic precautions must be followed when working with BCNU patients. The playlady should always be capped, gowned, masked and gloved; these protective garments are discarded immediately after leaving the unit and the hands thoroughly washed. Toys in the playroom require a regular cleaning. If an autoclave (gas oven) is accessible, it should be used. If not, each toy should be thoroughly washed down with either Micro-Bac® (an antiseptic cleaner) or alcohol before being given to a child. This is true also for "favorite" toys from home. The play area should be cleaned at least twice a day. Toys with wool—stuffed or furry animals—need to be removed from the play area and the patient's bedside. Wool and hair hold bacteria which can spread infection.

All toys, games and crafts should be screened for safety. New skin is especially sensitive; toys with sharp edges, pointed sticks, propelled objects (such as darts or bean shooters) or heating elements should be banned from the playroom. All toxic paints and glues, flammable arts and crafts materials such as gimp, crepe paper, oil base paints and thinners should not be ordered; most are available in nonflammable forms. Never give small children games or crafts materials with small beads or marbles unless strictly supervised, and one might hesitate even then because small hands are fast. In spite of these precautions, normal play can prevail. Children are resilient and can work out most of their differences. The playlady should intervene only if physical or severe emotional abuse is imminent.

The Ideal Playroom

There should be a corner in every institution that could be transformed into a spacious, clean, well-lighted "safe" place: the playroom. Ample floorspace provides the necessary room for free movement and equipment. Beds are a way of life in hospitals; the playroom should be able to accommodate beds and free play. The free movement area could be used for hopscotch, shuffleboard, bowling games (hand set), creative movement and dance. Equipment such as ping-pong tables, pool tables, perhaps even pinball machines, mini-gym sets and playhouses for tots, tricycles, and rocking horses add greatly to the program. A puppet stage, puppets, dolls, building blocks and a book corner are a necessity. Ample shelving and cabinet space for toys, games, and arts and crafts materials as well as the table space to use them cannot be overemphasized. Musical instruments and sound equipment coupled with television and access to a movie projector and screen complete the bare essentials for a "dream" playroom.

If at all possible, an additional area should be set aside for older patients. Teens appreciate the opportunity to escape toddlers and "kids." Sound equipment, tapes and records make this area a home away from home. More sophisticated crafts and materials may be kept here for the amusement of the teenager.

A pleasant outside area, green and well fenced in, makes a great extension to the playroom. If funds are available, safety-approved playground equipment and good weather are an unbeatable match.

The Play Program

The objectives of the therapeutic recreation program with burned children cannot be given in a complete listing. Hopefully, the program is flexible and adaptable to the individualized patient-care aim. However, the basic objectives are:

1. To provide enjoyment and diversion for the child who experiences a long-term stay in the hospital.
2. To supplement and complement the medical effort of the hospital team during the child's rehabilitation.
3. To aid in the social, psychological and emotional adjustment of the child.

The Burned Child

There is a challenge for the recreation therapist at each stage of the child's admission. Listed below are just a few of the problems facing the playlady during the initial stay of a patient. Since it would be impossible to list every challenge and its solution, one must follow the pattern of solving the problem and project solutions onto other limitations and disabilities.

The severely burned child is admitted to the hospital. He is extensively burned so he is placed in a BCNU. Usually the patient is too sick the first few days and is not interested in play or company. If the child is conscious, the playlady may introduce herself and explain to the child what she does in the hospital. This "stopping by" establishes a relationship with the child; a friendly face upon which he can rely.

When a child is restricted in bed without the use of his hands, the following solutions may be helpful:

1. Conversation (attention and tender loving care (TLC) are most helpful during this period of intense fear and frustration)
2. TV and movies
3. Reading stories; books or records from the library for the blind
4. Radio or phonograph
5. Word games, paper games, or puzzles (playlady moves for the patient in games)
6. Projects in arts and crafts made under the patient's direction
7. Make-believe
8. Singing
9. Sometimes a highly motivated child will paint or draw with feet or mouth.

When a child has limited use of one or both of his hands, the above list can be expanded to include:

1. Puppets
2. Box games
3. Coloring, arts and crafts
4. Beanbags
5. Bead projects
6. Books and comic books.

Games and projects can be devised to meet any challenge. All sports can be adapted so there is little need to list them. When at all possible, the child should be brought to the playroom by any mode of transportation available (bed, wheelchair, go-cart, walker). The children should be encouraged to come to the playroom. Through participating in group projects and free play the child
1. achieves self-satisfaction,
2. socializes, integrates and relates to others,
3. learns cooperation and sharing.

The physically limited patient should be aided in participating in the group project, or an individualized project should be devised for him.

Any excuse for a party—it is a good rule for the play program. Parties brighten up the monotony of a lengthy stay in the hospital—birthdays, holidays and parties for party's sake. Changing the atmosphere of the playroom is always refreshing. Perhaps one day the playroom could be converted into a zoo and all the patients are the animals. Another day could bring a carnival with special games and events.

The playroom should operate on regular hours when at all possible. The constancy is assuring to the patient. Some days, however, the playroom could be moved. Outdoor facilities in good weather are an excellent change of pace. Added supervision is usually necessary because the child tends to explode into movement after being indoors for so long. Well-known personalities and performing artists are always well received. These visits also change the nature of the playroom.

If volunteers are available, they always complement the play program. They should be carefully screened and oriented to the burn-play program. They serve several functions: each is a new face and another "safe" person, each can give special individualized attention to a patient who may need it (but is lacking it because the playlady must be with the group); they aid in the slow integration process with the world outside the hospital.

There is a great deal of apprehension on the part of the burned child when faced with the prospect of entering the world outside the hospital once again. "How will others react to me?"

The field trip aids in this part of the adjustment of a burned child. Trips to local museums, theaters and restaurants are not only fun but are a gradual integration into the outside world. These trips should be well-supervised on a one-to-one basis of patient to staff member or volunteer. In this way, should a traumatic moment occur, no other patient is left vulnerable.

The recreation therapist should have a good library of activities and crafts. This on-hand knowledge coupled with initiative and creativity will make a good workable program. At all times, a playlady must be flexible. She should not lose sight of the needs or wants of a group. If a planned activity is not working, drop it before the interest is lost. Honesty is of the essence. Burned children are so often patronized and pampered. Treat them as any other child, with candor and respect, and the relationship is made.

Conclusion

Searching through the want-ads, one comes across an ever-increasing demand for recreation therapists on hospital staffs. Perhaps, through this paper, one can adapt some of the methods used in a burn hospital to that of any institution where there are limitations of physical movement or bacteria control. Most of the theories and methods discussed in the paper can be adapted. Flexibility, imagination, freshness and understanding are the most important qualifications for a hospital recreation therapist. Patients are not detached entities or objects; they are real people with wants, needs, likes and dislikes which should be respected. Never losing sight of this fact, one is on his way to a successful play program.

BIBLIOGRAPHY

Burke, John F.: Modern burn therapy. *Sandoz Panorama*. November-December 1969, 4-11.

Flammable Fabrics. Third Annual Report to the President, 1971.

Hitchcock, C. R. and Horowitz, C.: Therapy of severely burned patients. *Arch Surg, LXXIV*:485-499, 1957.

Martin, Helen L., *et al:* The family of the fatally burned child. *Lancet II*:628-629, 1968.

Morgan, Alfred P. and Moore, F. D.: Answers to questions on burns, *Hosp Med, IV*:71-89, 1968.

Woodward, Joan: Emotional disturbances of burned children. *Br Med J,* *1:*1009-1013, 1959.

Additional Information from Shriner's Burn Institute.

"Semi-annual Report of the Play Therapy Department," Kathleen Lanza.

Lectures on Bacteria Control by Dr. John Burke, Chief of Staff, Shriner's Burn Institute, Boston.

Personal Interviews with Burnet Sumner, Psychiatric Social Worker, Shriner's Burn Institute, Boston. Dr. Norman Bernstein, Staff Psychiatrist, Shriner's Burn Institute, Boston.

CHAPTER 2

A PROGRAM FOR CHILDREN IN AN ACUTE HOSPITAL

JOYCE KOCZAN

WHEN CHILDREN ENTER a hospital, their entire emotional balance becomes disturbed. They are separated from their parents and friends, confined to a strange room, introduced to different people and sometimes subjected to painful procedures which they know little or nothing about. They become fearful and anxious. In order for them to maintain their equilibrium, they attempt to use an intricate system of defense and escape. The technique used by these hospitalized children is the same one used by nonhospitalized children—play.

Although the sense of play is expressed in a number of accepted definitions as "exercise or action for amusement; freedom, or scope for motion or action; freedom or abstinence from work,"[1] it is a manifestation of internal needs and wishes. Like work, it is a necessity, but one required to maintain a healthy balance and perspective in life. It is an end in itself that produces satisfaction. To hospitalized children, play achieves the goal of helping to release frustrations and anxieties in a socially acceptable manner. Children control the situations through their imagination and establish a perfect world in which they move from the known to the unknown.

Since World War II, largely because of increased knowledge of child development and medicine, there has been a change in the Pediatric units from being disease-oriented to patient-oriented. The total climate is still changing as those responsible for hospitalized children begin to recognize their needs.

Hospital personnel are not always aware of the frustrations,

---

1. Richard Dattner, *Design for Play.* New York, Van Nostrand Reinhold Co., 1969, p. 7.

threatening feelings, and new fears which confront hospitalized children. A discrepancy exists between their perceptions and goals and those of the patients. The doctor's goal of cure, rehabilitation, or both is often remote, while children's goals center on their current needs for pleasure. They want to be cured immediately and returned to their familiar and safe atmosphere of the home where they know their needs can be easily attained.

Since the latter is almost impossible, it is necessary for a hospital to meet the needs of the children through the establishment of an organized play program. One must realize that hospitalized children are not merely some sort of laboratory animal. They are people who have needs which must be satisfied, even though they are confined to a particular space. Hospital routine usually includes lengthy periods of free time in which no form of medical or other service is being performed. If meaningful activity is not provided, especially for immobilized children, lethargy, boredom, and low morale will result, in turn delaying the recovery process. When activities are provided, high morale will be reflected in the overall treatment outcome. Dr. Joseph B. Wolffe, Medical Director of the Valley Forge Heart and Medical Center stated:

> A survey of 1,000 patients has shown that carefully selected recreation to suit the patient's problem and personality resulted in the reduction of both drug requirements as well as length of hospital stay, when compared to the control group in the institution without the program.[2]

Children who have undergone or who are about to have serious operations are in need of a great deal of reassurance and support from everyone.

They have serious doubts about returning home as a complete person. The impersonality of the hospital does little to relieve their feelings of insecurity and concern. Play has the capacity for providing the kinds of activity and experiences that can restore feelings of personal worth.

---

2. Richard Kraus, *Recreation Today*. New York, Appleton-Century-Crofts. 1966, p. 305.

Children's Needs

Children's needs do not change simply because they are hospitalized. They are unique individuals who still possess needs for acceptance, love, warmth, affection, and understanding, not only from their parents, but from other adults. Only now, during hospitalization, these needs are increased. As Carlson, Deppe, and MacLean expounded:

> The ill and the handicapped still have the same need to belong, to create, to feel secure, to love and be loved, to feel significant, and to experience new adventure. The needs are the same, but they are accentuated through privation. The cerebral-palsied youngster with convulsive motor patterns needs acceptance as much as his pretty, well-coordinated sister. Though the afflicted child may not get recognition for beauty or for motor ability, he must have substitute experiences in which he can feel successful and accepted.[3]

The former statement also holds true in an acute hospital, where things move at such a fast rate that children have little time to understand what's happening. They need to know what is expected of them as well as the limits under which they can function.

All children, unless acutely ill physically or mentally, are active. They want to explore and find out about their surroundings and to discover something of interest. For this they must have some space, materials and equipment, no matter how simple. Children learn from others beside their parents, and develop a sense of trust or mistrust depending upon their experiences with adults.

Since the hospital is a very threatening place to children, they need someone other than the parents whom they can trust when the parents are absent. Someone who can help them better cope with the medical procedures and with their emotions in the hospital. This includes being able to express their feelings when the need arises as well as controlling both positive and negative feelings. Fear and anger are present in all children. They need help in coping with these feelings and in finding suitable outlets for

---

3. *Ibid.*

them. Children need to play and proper recreation activity will reduce child tension while at the same time provide a more pleasant climate for the nursing personnel.

Meeting Needs Through Play

The basic needs of children have not always been recognized in hospitals because of the fact that the primary goal of hospitalization was to save lives. This primary goal still exists, but, because of advanced medicine and increased understanding of child development, strict visiting hours, prolonged bed rest, extended hospitalization, and rigidly enforced rules are becoming a thing of the past. In the present-day hospital, parents are being welcomed at all hours, the average stay is a brief one, and the needs of hospitalized children are slowly being met. One of the ways the children are benefiting is through the establishment of organized play programs, conducted under the supervision of professional people.

Play was formerly considered necessary only for the disturbed child who was in need of play therapy. Today, play holds the connotation of being a child's work, the means through which he learns, the way he spends most of his time.

In an organized play program, the hospitalized child has the opportunity to grow and learn through physical activity, intellectual stimulation, socialization, and emotional release. Play also helps the child better understand the medical procedure to which he will be subjected. No matter how crude the play activity may seem to an observer, if it satisfies the child it is therapeutically sound. The primary concern is not the finished product but rather the process of involvement and the fact that he is doing something on his own. In order for the hospitalized child to become personally involved in play he must have space, freedom to play without constant interruption, and adequate materials. The playroom is the one area in the hospital where children should be given the freedom to choose for themselves the type of activity or inactivity in which they want to participate.

The Hospital Play Program

In planning a program for children in an acute hospital, one will quite often hear such phrases as "administration and nursing service feel we're wasting time if we play with the children." Or, "the idea sounds good, but the hospital can't afford play equipment." Or, "we need all the available rooms for patients." Or, "you're going to cross-contaminate the patients." One will be pulled in many directions by such negative attitudes. It takes time, planning, organization and determination to provide a play program, but it can and should be established in every hospital. Nursing service and administrative personnel must be fundamentally convinced that children do need play, even in the hospital, and that play will reduce tensions for both child and nursing staff while also serving to hasten recovery. They should be convinced that play is as important to the attitude adjustment and general welfare of the hospitalized child as a proper diet and clean quarters. The hospital play program is an integral part of total patient care and should be so recognized.

The play area should be the center of activity. Ideally, it should be easily accessible to the patients with an outdoor area close by and all equipment flexible and mobile. In most acute hospitals, the play area is a small room at the end of the corridor out of the mainstream of traffic. Simplicity of design should be a key consideration. The room should be large enough to accommodate wheelchairs, IV poles, and stretchers. It should be equipped for use by the children and not as a showroom for parents. When no space is available, play should take place within the patient unit. This has advantages because the children on bed rest, or those who are too ill to participate actively will gain confidence in knowing that normal life is going on around them, even though they are unable to join the group. Playing within the patient unit also stimulates the depressed or frightened children who are often scared to come to the playroom for fear that their mothers won't find them. Membership in a group also helps to increase the confidence of children who must undergo treatments which other children have already experienced.

A playroom allows for better supervision of the children and also serves as an ideal observation area for the medical staff. Here children are observed in a relaxed setting where their behavior is more natural.

Although space standards for recreation in the hospital setting have not been formalized, there should be an ample open area in which the children can work, move, and explore beyond that which is required for cabinet, sink, and supply space.

Another consideration is the opportunity to play without constant interruption. Hospital schedules are structured so that the major medical procedures and doctor visitations usually occur in the early morning hours, leaving the remainder of the time for play. The children who are scheduled for surgery are less apprehensive when allowed to play before they are sedated. The play group will shift as children come and go between procedures, but it is a continuing experience. When children must be interrupted for a medical reason they are more cooperative because they know they can return. Play is therapeutic when such activities as dramatic play or doctor and hospital play occur where the children act out what will be happening to them using authentic articles as bandages, syringes and stethoscopes on dolls. Having their favorite toy from home enables the children to feel more confident while in the hospital.

Equipping a Playroom

Play equipment and supplies need not be elaborate but they must be safe and suitable. Such equipment might include sandboxes, climbing apparatus, pull toys, riding toys, provisions for water play, dolls and doll houses, books, games, puzzles, and art materials. Interested citizens, organizations and local manufacturing firms can be encouraged to provide sturdy toys for use in the hospital, many of which could later be recycled. Materials essential for any playroom are those which allow freedom of imagination and promote play activity. These include:

Blocks—Variations in size for small children to intricate blocks for older children with different shapes and colors.
Clay—Molding clay or play dough (can be made from flour, salt, water) can be beaten, pulled, punched, baked or painted.
Paints—Finger and brush paints give insight to a child's feelings.
Water—Soothing for children; can be provided in colored containers for pouring or bubble blowing.
Sandbox—Used wet or dry for group or individual play; sand stimulates the tactile sense.

In addition to these materials, cooking experiences, crayons and coloring books, scissors and colored paper are basic for daily activity. Probably one of the most popular play materials made by the children is play dough. They enjoy the measuring and mixing of the ingredients as well as the pounding, shaping, creating and destroying of their projects. Such an activity keeps the children actively involved for extended periods of time. One can often observe anger being displayed during play sessions in the forms of pounding or throwing the play dough, scrubbing frantically with a paint brush, or knocking down a block construction. These activities provide a safety valve for pent-up emotions reducing anger and fear. Children also delight in helping out with the materials or in assisting bedridden patients with projects. Children confined to bed with an IV during a play session will very often test adult ingenuity by asking for materials to which they can create games or vicarious play within their limitations.

Staffing and Administration

Without skillful guidance, all space, time, and equipment for play can be misused. A well-organized viable play program is only as strong as those responsible for it. Increasingly the need for professional training and experience is being recognized. Not all well-trained people are comfortable in a hospital setting.

Few standards have yet been established, because of the newness of therapeutic play programs. Persons with either a recreation education background, or elementary education, seem to be best suited for the position as play leader. The personnel department should be informed of this so that the best qualified can be hired. Knowledge of child development and experience in working with children are necessary, but basic to all requirements should be a genuine enjoyment in working with young children, skill in relating to them, and an ability to work under the stress which occurs in hospitals. Other qualities which should be considered before appointing a play leader are objectivity in meeting individual needs, the ability to handle difficult and aggressive children, and creativity in guiding and motivating children to discover suitable recreational pursuits.

Volunteers and students, who need a brief orientation, are important in contributing to a more comprehensive program. They may be asked to lead activities, supervise the play area during the evening and weekend hours or in the absence of the play leader. Some of the appropriate toys and equipment should be stored so that the nursing staff might conduct some activities in the event that the leader is busy or when the need arises. In-service education is necessary in order to keep nursing personnel alert to children's play needs. Administration must also become aware of the needs of the play area and provide allocations to properly equip it. The recreation therapist frequently will supplement the budget and seek donations from local resources. Interested citizens and organizations will welcome the opportunity to provide some of the needed equipment if they are properly approached.

In planning and financing a play program, some criteria for consideration are the following:

Salary (comparative with teachers, nurses, social workers), office space, secretarial services, storage space, a budget based on patient/year formula, equipment (tables, chairs, piano, projector, record player, etc.); expendable supplies, repair of equipment, travel and conference expenses, education and resource materials, and donations (being able to accept outside donations for program without turning money into the hospital).

A well-organized play program serves as a diagnostic tool, as well as being therapeutic, especially with children who have a functional illness. Much can be learned by watching children at play. Written observations can be helpful to the medical and paramedical staff. How the child uses materials, his relationship to people, his ability to cope with medical procedures, and his attitude about being in the hospital are important to record. The playroom can also be used as a teaching tool for students. Observing and discussing a child's behavior during hospitalization will reveal his reactions under extraordinary conditions and circumstances, thus offering a new perspective of the child's ability to adapt and adjust.

In essence, a play program in an acute hospital does more than merely divert and entertain hospitalized children. It is a continuum in the child's normal growth and development pattern.

It should be considered as an integral part of optimum pediatric care, an important factor in a child's hospital experience. Play is not a cure-all, and its direct benefits have not as yet been sufficiently researched; however, immediate reaction to the program will come from its participants—the children, and from those closest to the participants—their parents. Can't we all learn something from them?

Some typical comments by children about the therapeutic play program are: "I never knew the hospital was so much fun." "Can I stay another day to finish my project?" "What are we going to do tomorrow?"

Comments heard by parents are: "This is really great for the children." "If I had known she was having this much fun, I wouldn't have rushed to get here so early." "Every hospital should have a program like this."

BIBLIOGRAPHY

Dattner, Richard: *Design for Play.* New York, Van Nostrand Reinhold Co., 1969.

Kraus, Richard: *Recreation Today.* New York, Appleton-Century-Crofts, 1966.

CHAPTER 3

CASE STUDY OF A DISABLED VETERAN

Michael Sorter

It was on a hot day in July of 1968, that the war ended for Kevin Joyce, and his life changed for all time. Behind him were the carefree times of a 21-year-old youth—the gaiety, the sports, the joy of just being young—ahead lay only pain, handicap, adjustments, and frustration. Granted that Kevin's history is not at all a rare happening in the annals of the wounded veteran, I found him to have so much to offer as a person, as a returned soldier, as one of the unsung heroes, as a counselor, as a husband and father, and as an example of sheer determination, that I felt I would like to make known my impression of this remarkable young man.

Kevin was born January 21, 1947, in Worcester, Massachusetts. In every sense of the word, his childhood and growing-up years were completely natural and normal. He was a healthy boy, with the usual round of accidents and diseases, but nothing that would help equip him for the long months of suffering he would later endure. After graduating from high school, Kevin went to work for General Motors for a year before deciding to further his education. He chose Murray State College in Tishmingo, Oklahoma and completed two years successfully. During his junior year he was drafted into the Army.

Upon completion of basic training and advanced individual training, Kevin was sent to Vietnam. He was assigned as squad leader with the U. S. Army Infantry, First Mobile Cavalry Division. During a mission to secure the rice harvest near Quang Tri Province the platoon was under fire from the North Vietnamese. As his squad advanced on the dug-in position of the Vietcong, an electronically detonated mine exploded, blowing off both Kevin's legs below the knee. He had been in Vietnam for four months.

Kevin was immediately evacuated to a medical aid station where the medics labored feverishly to stop the bleeding. He was then transferred to a hospital where he was prepared for surgery and remained conscious for the first three hours of his long and arduous ordeal. After two weeks of postoperative care at a military hospital in Japan he was transferred to a hospital in the United States with a Bronze Star, an Air Medal, a Combat Infantry Badge, two Purple Hearts, and two useless stumps for legs.

Twenty-five months of hospitalization and rehabilitation became his life, seven months at Valley Forge Hospital in Pennsylvania, and one and a half years at the West Roxbury V.A. Hospital in Massachusetts. During his stay at Valley Forge, Kevin endured several of his thirteen operations. Approximately five or six were attempts to save his knees as it is much easier to wear a prosthesis if the knee remains. In Kevin's case, however, it was impossible to do so since he had developed osteomyelitis, an infection of the bone marrow. Kevin refers to his last operation as "lucky thirteen" and is quick to note that most double leg amputees normally do not require so many. His operations became necessary, however, due to infections and complications. As soon as his healed legs indicated readiness he was declared able to participate in a program of rehabilitation.

In talking about his long struggle to overcome discouragement and despair, Kevin commented: "You spend that much time in the hospital, and you see guys a lot worse off than you are. You don't really want to die, so you adjust—you learn to live with your disability—you adjust, or become a vegetable, because nothing in the world is going to change your physical situation." Kevin decided to keep going.

In order to manage a prosthesis, or even a wheelchair, he had to strengthen his upper torso since "just to get enough power to wheel around was an effort at first." But he tried continuously and with the help of therapeutic specialists he exercised constantly. To strengthen arm muscles push-ups in the wheelchair were recommended. He used the arms of his chair for support and this became a daily ritual. There were stump exercises to prepare his legs for prosthesis and stretching exercises to keep from geting muscle contractions. After many weeks of practice and hard work, using the parallel bars and his prosthesis, Kevin became proficient enough to use the artificial legs with crutches. While at West Roxbury V.A. he also learned to walk, this time with a gait specifically designed to his condition and abilities. "I got pretty good with the artificial legs. I was walking with one cane on the wards but stairs were still difficult to manage."

Adjusting oneself physically is only one phase of the rehabilitation program. There is also a need for mental and emotional readjustments; to relax, to learn new leisure interests, to overcome feelings of being different and to gain new confidence. Recreational therapy provided a strong influence here. One becomes proficient at chess and other quiet games which had been previously ignored. These activities also promote social interaction which is desperately needed. Kevin found a new interest in painting and music and benefited by the satisfactions of developing some skill in these areas. "My happiest surprise was that I could still swim. It was difficult at first to discover that a loss of legs had changed my center of gravity. I was actually more buoyant and had to compensate in swimming by using a shorter arm stroke to go with my short stump kick, but it worked."

Following discharge from West Roxbury V.A., Kevin decided to finish his education. Entering the University of Massachusetts he successfully completed his senior year on the GI bill. Subsequently, he married his sweetheart, Linda, which wasn't exactly a planned phase of his rehabilitation program yet a very valuable input. A new life was shaping with its responsibilities and privileges; he now had to find suitable employment. A Job Mart, sponsored by the V.A. and the Division of Employment Security which consisted of firms interested in employing disabled persons, was brought to Kevin's attention. He wheeled himself in to be interviewed by personnel managers of various companies and agencies. "I didn't know what or who I was looking for at this point—I was just determined to find a job." The first booth he visited was that of the Veterans Administration. A job opportunity counseling veterans appealed to his sense of performing a useful service and he felt confident of his ability to do the job. A few months later, with Civil Service tests behind him, Kevin went to work for the V.A. He now sits at a desk in a large office on the fifth floor of the John F. Kennedy Building in Boston. His job is to provide information, referral and counseling service to veterans by telephone. It is a new concept. Previously veterans waited a long time for service, when often they had only one question which could have been answered easily by telephone. Kevin says, "It's a satisfying job. I feel that I am contributing something, especially to guys who are as handicapped as I was." At work he still has the artificial legs, but does not use them very often; for getting up, sitting down and maneuvering around is easier to accomplish in the wheelchair.

Kevin and his family live in Framingham now, and every morning he puts the wheelchair into his specially equipped car and drives to work. As a contact representative he mans a busy information telephone, explaining benefits to veterans, telling them how to expedite their claims and relating to them in a most personal way since he is one of them. As he said, "I keep wondering how a guy like me, with physical limitations, ever hoped to help less fortunate veterans and their families—but I can." He further expressed his feeling for the annual "hire the handicapped" week. "This observance has a special meaning to me because it was through this promotion that I got my big opportunity."

Kevin has developed a philosophy for all handicapped people —that one must totally accept one's self with the handicap, or there is nothing. He feels that public attitudes are the greatest threat to rehabilitation. Perhaps people are well-meaning, but generally they have not learned to accept those who are impaired. The general public is oversolicitous, overprotective and unwilling to give the disabled a chance to do things for themselves. Handicapped people want neither pity nor special treatment because this promotes a psychological handicap in addition to the physical disability. Kevin is grateful for the therapy which helped to remold his body, mind and spirit. It helped to bring him back to the active world. As a husband, a father, a sufficient wage earner and a man with adequate leisure skills, Kevin is able to live life to the fullest. In the purest sense of the word, he is again a whole man.

SECTION II

THE MENTALLY RETARDED

Courtesy of Recreation Department
City of Quincy
Massachusetts

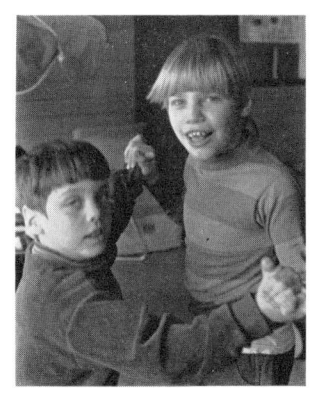

Courtesy of Charles V.
Hogan Regional Center
Town of Danvers
Massachusetts

CHAPTER 4

HOGAN REGIONAL CENTER: A SCHOOL FOR THE RETARDED

CHRISTINE KONIECZNY

THE CHARLES V. HOGAN REGIONAL CENTER, located in Danvers, Massachusetts, is a comprehensive facility serving the mentally retarded from 42 towns in the northeastern corner of the Commonwealth (Region IV). Hogan, formerly called Hathorne Regional Center is the infant among the five state schools, the first patient having been admitted in January of 1967.

> During this period the Massachusetts Mental Retardation Planning Project selected Hogan as the Commonwealth's instrument for developing a comprehensive program for the mentally retarded.
> The report titled "Massachusetts Plans for Its Retarded—a Ten Year Plan" has been the bible of this institution in the development of services, staffing patterns and internal organizational structure.[1]

The year 1966 saw the passing of the Comprehensive Mental Health and Retardation Services Act. This act divided the Department of Mental Health into thirty-nine geographical areas, each including 75,000 to 200,000 residents, and it organized the state into seven new regions.[2]

Citizen participation in the problems of mental retardation was invited from the beginning and has helped to influence the philosophy of Hogan.[3] Under the guidance by Dr. Karel J. de Haas, the first pediatrician to serve as superintendent in the Massachusetts Department of Mental Health, the philosophy of this pioneering program at Hogan developed.

---

1. James W. Oien, "A State School's Philosophy and the Occupational Therapist's Related Role," presented at Hathorne State School, 1968.
2. Massachusetts Department of Mental Health, *Challenge and Response*. Massachusetts, 1973, p. 11.
3. Oien, *Op. Cit.*, p. 2.

1. To maintain a child within his family, realizing at the same time the problems inherent to family care of the retarded.
2. The Center should strive for full coordination and cooperation even to the extent of merger with existing facilities or agencies within the community....
3. Finding alternatives to residential care whenever possible should be the major objective.
4. A full range of services should be provided according to the treatment needs of the individual....
5. Continuity of care....[4]

> To be a comprehensive community mental retardation center, a facility must include at least eight essential elements: preventive, diagnostic and evaluation services, treatment services, training services, educational services, personal care services as well as prevocational, vocational and recreational. Hogan has developed these maximum services.[5]

"Although Hogan was designed as a residential school, requests for day care service outnumber requests for residential services by four to one. Many parents who initially requested residence have been able to maintain their child at home, because of family supportive services."[6] The Community Evaluation and Rehabilitation Center screens candidates and helps place them in appropriate programs in the community or, if necessary, in the institution. There are a variety of arrangements such as long- and short-term patient care, day care, half-day programs, partial-week live-in programs and special residential care....[7] From Region IV 180 day students and 300 residential students utilize the center. In addition, approximately 500 cases receive community guidance or outpatient services. Clients are at varying levels of retardation and may have speech, hearing or ambulatory problems as well.

Unitization

The school is divided into separate wings, designated as units, which are connected by corridors to the recreational and training

---

4. *Ibid.*, p. 2, 3.
5. *Ibid.*, p. 3.
6. *Ibid.*, p. 4.
7. Department of Mental Health, *Op. Cit.*, p. 89.

centers. The four units divide the residential population according to age and nursing care requirements. The units are as follows: the infirmary, those who require a minimum of 75 percent nursing care; the nursery, ages ten and under; the adolescents, ages eleven through eighteen; and adults, age nineteen and over. Each unit has its own unit supervisor who is assisted by a multi-disciplined staff. Staff personnel include:

social service	nursing
speech and hearing therapists	dentistry
recreation therapists	medicine
occupational therapists	psychology
music therapists	rehabilitation
physical therapists	special education
attendants or aides	

The team approach is used in formulating a program for each child. A student's progress is reviewed annually through school reports, progress notes and case conferences. Each unit also develops its own program which is designed to suit its individual needs. The training and recreation centers service these units.

Training Center

The training center includes classrooms and workshops. In addition, it houses hair salons for men and women, a student lounge, a regional library and a gift shop.

"The Education Department is a service providing structured classroom learning for students over five years of age."[8] The department's primary concern is to eliminate or substantially reduce the learning disability which prevents a child from receiving public school placement. The most predominant technique used is that of behavior modification. The school program is divided into:

Pre-nursery	Adults
Nursery	Deaf retarded
Early elementary	Physically handicapped

Classes are held daily from 9:00 A.M. to 3:00 P.M. September to

---

8. From unpublished data by Hogan Regional Center concerning the Education Department, May, 1973.

June. The staff consists of a principal, head teacher, music therapists, and twelve classroom teachers, plus additional positions added yearly through Federal grants. Educational centers also function within the nursery and adult units.

"The vocational independence program has as its goal trainee independence and self-initiation of tasks as well as further improvement of work habits and social skills."[9] Emphasis is less on production than on work habits. This program provides training for residential and day student adolescents and adults who meet specified requirements. "Within the program exists three phases of training: Initial exposure and vocational orientation, transition-preparation and training for work, extended training and maintenance, preparation for a sheltered workshop environment or community referral."[10]

Many of the products constructed at the center are sold in the gift shop or have been commissioned by private companies. Many students are reimbursed for their labors. In the near future, courses in community concepts (time, travel, etc.) will be added for adults.

Recreation Center

The philosophy of the recreation department is in accord with that of the Regional Center: the return of residents to the community, with emphasis on the acquisition of skills which would enable them to participate in community-sponsored recreation. The department also assists local communities in developing suitable recreation programs for people who are retarded.

The recreation staff consists of seventeen recreational therapists and a supervisor. Eleven of these positions are permanent with the remainder being filled by co-op students from Northeastern University. Each therapist is assigned a permanent position; five are assigned to the pool, two to the gymnasium and the remainder to the units. In addition, there are three student helpers and a daily average of ten volunteers.

---

9. From unpublished data by the Hogan Regional Center concerning the Rehabilitation Department Training Program, May 1973, p. 1.

10. *Ibid.*, p. 6.

Approximately 90 percent of the Center's population is served by the recreation center. The more severely disabled or retarded receive instruction in the specially equipped gross motor rooms located in each unit which are daily used by the physical therapists. Gross motor and behavior modification training is provided until the students are capable of attending the classes located within the recreation center.

The recreation center consists of a pool, gymnasium, bowling alleys, gross motor rooms in each unit and outdoor playgrounds. In addition, arts and crafts rooms are located in the training center and an auditorium is available for departmental use.

Program

The recreation program reaches out in an effort to serve the population within the areas of therapeutic, swimming, afternoon-evening programs, special activities and summer camping.

The therapeutic day program (9:00-3:00) is primarily physical in content and structure. Student participation is determined by the classroom schedule of the training center. Grouping is therefore based on educational rather than physical capabilities which result in physical and age variations. Classes are co-educational and students are seen on the average of twice a week for one-half to one hour sessions. The introduction of new activities is based upon student progress. Quarterly reports on the progress of each child are filed by the recreation staff. Activities offered in the therapeutic day program include the following organized sports:

basketball	shuffleboard
street hockey	volleyball
softball	badminton and
bowling	high or low organization games.

Gymnastics is popular, particularly trampoline and tumbling. Additional therapeutic activities are exercises, movement exploration, body awareness through musical games, gross motor activity, parachute play, nature exploration, music activities for adults, action songs and folk dancing.

The therapeutic day program ends with the departure of the day students and the afternoon-evening segment begins for those students energetic enough to participate.

Swimming is a vital part of the daily recreational program. Instruction is offered one hour per week to each unit with the actual time determined by the recreation therapists in the unit and the classroom teachers. Because transportation and dressing time is included, water time is reduced to one-half hour. Class size varies from individual instruction to a class of 15 to 20 swimmers. Class activities range from hydrotherapy conducted in consultation with the physical therapists to lessons for a Red Cross advanced beginner. Free swim time is available during the afternoons, evenings (twice a week until 9:00 p.m.), and on Saturdays, for independent residents who are capable of ambulation. The residents who require assistance in reaching the pool are assigned times for informal instruction during this free swim time. Indoor and outdoor wading pools are also available for water adjustment and free play.

The afternoon-evening program is less structured and more recreational in nature. Some of the activities offered are organized intramurals, playground activity, and club groups. Hobby clubs are provided by the Center and also open to retarded people in adjacent communities. Popular club groups include bicycling, cheerleading, Brownies, Boy Scouts, nature, a community social club and ski club. The student lounge is open to independent residents for socialization, record playing, and ping-pong. Included in the special activities program are special events and field trips to such places as sporting events, Museum of Science, music theater, Aquarium and the zoo. Field trips have been facilitated by the acquisition of a regular-sized bus adapted for the handicapped and a mini-bus. Participation in the daily field trips is determined by units and student interest. The day students are invited to participate in some of the special events such as the indoor ice skating, monthly birthday parties, dances and outings. Special Olympics and the training that goes into it is an annual special activity of far-reaching proportions.

A summer day camp has been established at the Hogan Regional Center for both day and resident students. Day students are asked to initially seek out community camps, but if unable to do so are admitted to the school camp. In addition, thirty residents are placed in community playgrounds and 116 attend a residential camp in Amesbury which was developed as the result of a Federal grant, coordinated with the Hawthorne Girl Scouts of Danvers. Key staff positions are filled by Center personnel and additional positions are added through grants.

Community Involvement

The recreation center emphasizes the need for community involvement. It urges local towns to establish new programs or to extend already existing ones. The day students benefit most from such programs as several towns have initiated summer day camps, Saturday programs, and clubs in which these special students may participate.

Many local service groups have contributed time and funds to the Center. These funds have been used by the recreation department to purchase equipment. Private businesses have also provided the use of their facilities at no charge or at a reduced rate.

Families of the students are often invited to participate in activities such as swimming, cookouts, and the annual prom. This arrangement also provides an opportunity for parents to become more involved and to engage in parent therapy.

Implications

With the passage of the Special Education Act of 1972 and the resultant absorption of these students into the community schools, the population of the Center will alter. In the opinion of Mrs. Patricia Lindstrom, supervisor of recreation, in five to ten years the Center will care for a more specialized clientele— the deaf retardate, the blind retardate and the more severely retarded, while mildly retarded individuals become community based. The passage of law 766 in the Commonwealth which becomes effective September 1, 1974 will guarantee the integration of handicapped and retarded children in regular schools. The big question is, will they be accepted in the schools and the community?

The expansive program and efforts at the Hogan Regional Center has paved the way for moving in this direction.

BIBLIOGRAPHY

Massachusetts Department of Mental Health: *Challenge and Response*. Massachusetts, 1973.

Oien, James W.: A new state school's philosophy and the occupational therapist's related role. Presented at Hathorne State School, 1968.

Hogan Regional Center concerning the Education Department. May 1973.

Hogan Regional Center concerning the Rehabilitation Department Training Program. May, 1973.

CHAPTER 5

DAY CAMPING FOR THE RETARDED

EARL E. VERMILLION AND CHARLES L. ALONGI, JR.

RECREATION PROGRAMS for the mentally retarded children of Quincy, Massachusetts were launched in the summer of 1956. A pilot project was initiated at that time in a "small tot area" of a city playground. Two leaders were assigned to conduct a program for eight trainable retardates and transportation was provided by parents. This original program consisted of playground activities including simple games, crafts, singing, rhythm band, parties, swimming instruction, nature hikes and field trips. The program was an immediate success and led to the organization of a similar "winter program" held in a gymnasium on Saturday mornings for 25 weeks during the following school year.

The day camp program had its start in the summer of 1963. The Joseph F. Kennedy, Jr. Foundation awarded the Quincy Recreation Department a grant of 3000 dollars on a matching funds basis, for each year of a two-year period. Pageant Field, city owned property consisting of ten acres, was selected as the day camp site. Construction of facilities and cleaning of land was a joint project of the Quincy Park Department and the U. S. Army Reserves. Twenty-five campers and a staff of three plus 20 teenage volunteers constituted the total personnel for that original day camp season. This has grown to the 1973 totals of 80 campers, a staff of 16—all teachers or college students—plus over 100 registered teenage volunteers.

The camp facilities include two enclosed shelters, one for office purposes and the other for camper's personal gear and camp equipment. A large playground area is located near the shelters and this same general area serves as a meeting place for the various camper groups. An open-sided picnic shelter near the office is available for arts and crafts projects and quiet activities. The picnic shelter is surrounded by an expanse of concrete slab.

Fronting this area is a one-third mile blacktop oval enclosing two softball diamonds. On the far side of the oval is a professional horseshoe court and a boccie court. On the same side of the shelter is an open area sufficient for many games and large group activities and this is bounded by permanent rest room facilities. A natural salt-water lagoon is located two hundred yards away and it is there that the Quincy Recreation small craft program is held. Boating and sailing is available for the use of campers. Many trails, marshlands and wooded areas are also available on the perimeter.

The 80 campers are placed in one of eight groups on the basis of a subjective evaluation that includes ability to function as well as relative age and size. Two groups are composed of younger children up to ten years of age, the youngest camper being four and one-half years old. There are two groups of girls and two groups of boys from nine years to sixteen years of age, divided further into active and passive groups. The remaining two groups are for older persons (unlimited age—oldest, in 1973, being 78 years) also divided into active and passive groups.

Camp activities are as similar as possible to regular day camp activities for able-bodied youngsters. The philosophy has always been to be as normal as possible with the thought of trying any activity (adapted as is necessary) and to evaluate its success or failure. If successful, it would be retained and if a failure, it would be put aside for further possible use and assessment. The social values of children working and playing in groups is of prime importance in selecting activities. Even though individual activities necessary for physical and mental growth are often scheduled for younger children, the main impetus is toward group interaction.

Some of the more popular activities for retarded children include:

Trampoline: The trampoline is often, and rightly so, considered too dangerous for retarded children. However, with proper controls such as no flips, etc. it is valuable for its potential in developing body awareness, spatial relations and physical coordination. Even though children are restricted to simple stunts and routines, it has proven to be one of the all-time favorite activities. The same can be said of simple and basic tumbling activities.

Archery: This is another potentially dangerous activity that can only be justified if proper controls are present. The children quickly adapt to the rules and safety aspects of the sport. They may miss the target frequently, but the excitement expressed on any hit—especially a bull's eye—makes the day a success for the camper. Alternate target faces—including animal pictures or balloons—make the archery period more exciting.

Boccie and Horseshoes: These are two activities that are easy enough for campers of any age since they can be adapted to meet practically any need. Each can be conducted as a highly competitive activity or strictly as a social event. The older and the more passive campers are especially interested in participation stressing sociability.

Cricket: An Englishman might not recognize this game as cricket since it is really a combination of cricket and baseball. The degree of competition depends on the groups involved in the game. The value is in its simplicity. The pitcher is throwing at a physical object (the wicket) rather than an imaginary strike zone. The batter is merely trying to hit the ball and protect the wicket rather than make a split second decision of a strike or ball. Also, the base runner has only one place to run and the fielder only two places to make a play on a runner. It is an excellent lead-up to softball.

Floor Hockey: The enthusiasm for hockey has certainly been the result of the coverage of professional hockey on television, but its enthusiastic reception is also partly the result of Special Olympics competition. The campers seem to have a general understanding of the game and adapt to fundamentals and position play perhaps better than many other team sports. They also seem to have professional heroes in hockey more so than in other sports. Girls take pleasure and do better in floor hockey than in other team sports.

Boating and Sailing: We can definitely include boating and sailing among the dangerous activities that require considerable controls. Teenage volunteers from both the boating and sailing staff and the camp staff are imperative to the program. Camp volunteers are offered special lessons to prepare them for this responsibility. The instructional phase of the program for campers is generally restricted to rowing and seldom to sailing. However, campers do have a chance to "go for a sailboat ride" with an experienced sailor.

Folk Dance and Record Hops: Interest in music and talent in basic rhythmic movement in a nondirected manner seems to come naturally to most campers. Such activity certainly seems to be most pleasurable for them. Freedom in expression to current popular music elicits a dancing response found among any teenage group. Simple folk dancing of various cultures including American square dancing has been popular. Demonstrations of folk dancing by many campers has been a highlight of the past three or four Parents' Night programs.

Dramatics: Drama has not played a major role in our program to date and could be utilized more extensively. The younger groups use educational records and music in a dramatic type of free expression. They have also performed in simple skits involving "short lines" for each individual. Older campers have performed in short, adapted forms of plays such as *Snow White and the Seven Dwarfs* which was especially written for them by staff members or teenage volunteers. Such performances are usually prepared for presentation at Parents' Night.

Overnight Camping: Overnight camp-outs are provided twice per session—once for boys and once for girls. The program is of a relaxed nature rather than highly structured. An enjoyable evening and a night away from home is the desirable goal. Preparation of the evening meal and enjoyable recreational pursuits plus a lot of talking and trying to stay awake all night are important to the camper but somewhat trying on the staff. The morning consists of a simple breakfast, packing and clean-up duties.

Frisbee Golf: The most recent innovation of the 1973 season was frisbee golf. The idea is to throw the frisbee as many times as is necessary to hit a plastic cone. The number of throws required to hit the cone constitutes the score for that hole. The distance between the holes varies from about 20 to 75 yards. The course is also set up to include obstacles such as bushes, benches or backstops. This game was completely new, and proved to be extremely popular.

Special Olympics: The premier activity for the past six years has been Special Olympics competition. To our knowledge, Quincy Recreation was the first organization in the East to conduct a Special Olympics program. It has grown beyond being just a summer activity and now consists of a year-round program involving not only Quincy Recreation but the Quincy Public Schools, the Quincy Junior College, and the Quincy Jaycees. Quincy children have competed in six Quincy Special Olympics, two Norfolk County, two Boston Invitational, four Massachusetts and two International (Chicago and Los Angeles) Special Olympics. Approximately 125 to 140 Quincy children have competed over the six-year period. Special Olympics originally offered only track and field competition but now has been expanded to include swimming, basketball, floor hockey, volleyball and gymnastics.

Other activities include most team sports and individual activities of a physical nature. Arts and crafts is important and the philosophy might be stated as: "Let the camper complete a project that is worthy of display at home so that parents will keep it for its value or attractiveness rather than just keeping the project to build an ego for their child."

Every retarded person in the city of Quincy is eligible to register as a camper. Age is not considered a particular problem (age range in 1973 was four and one-half to seventy-eight years). The one firm requirement is that the camper must be toilet trained and basically able to care for his own personal needs. Beyond that, we feel that we can program and instruct to such a degree that each child will have a rewarding and meaningful experience. The Recreation Department maintains up-to-date rosters of past campers but the Quincy Public Schools also furnish a complete listing of special education students each year. Registration and medical forms plus a letter concerning the camp is sent to each family during the spring of the year. Follow-up telephone calls are made to families not responding. The campers are basically recruited through this procedure, but a few new campers each year are often enrolled through word-of-mouth efforts on the part of friends of the camp.

Teenage volunteers, the absolute backbone of the camp, are recruited through the cooperation of the Quincy Public Schools and the parochial schools in the city. Quincy Recreation personnel associated with the camp conduct assembly programs in each of the schools. Interested students then register as volunteers and render service as their time permits during the summer. Usually this is a full-time project for the volunteer and as a full-time volunteer he or she is most valuable to the camp. Part-time volunteers are kept to a minimum.

A three-day training program for volunteers is conducted prior to the opening of camp. The volunteers are made aware of the different types of handicaps and varying degrees of retardation they might meet. The major portion of the training consists of learning to participate in all the camp activities and how to help a camper in a one-to-one relationship in these activities. We try to impress upon the volunteer that the camp is only as good as they make it. Volunteers get directions from the professional staff but ultimately the success of the program is in their hands because they are the consultant, friend, teacher and frequently confidant to the campers assigned to them.

The basic reward for the volunteer is a sense of accomplishment and an opportunity to evaluate himself as to his worth in this or a related field as a vocation in life. Recognition of their job is expressed in more immediate terms by various special programs designed strictly for the volunteers such as beach parties, cookouts, dances or trips to amusement parks. They are also eligible for Quincy Recreation Junior Leader Awards, certificates of merit from United Community Services and the Elk's Youth Awards.

The professional staff is selected from among many applicants for the specific position of day camp counselor. The applicants are in such number that staff members are selected among college graduates and teachers or at least college students majoring in special education or recreation. Staff members who were previously teenage volunteers number as high as 60 to 75 percent of the total. The 1973 staff of 16 persons represent a total of 70 years' service to the camp.

The 1973 season saw a new innovation in day camping for the retarded. We can no longer call it a children's camp because of the extension of the age range to include the elderly retarded. We were aware that patients at the various state institutions were being returned to the city and often placed in nursing homes. We were surprised, but pleased to locate twelve such potential campers by recruiting through the nursing homes. Living in the nursing home was certainly adequate and the surroundings pleasant. The residents were well cared for, but life was just a simple routine existence. The nursing administrators leaped at the chance to enroll elderly retarded people in camp, and the patients were excited about the prospect. The camp staff was apprehensive about the new group and concerned about programming and safety. As it developed, several of our established, less active campers were placed in the same group with the patients. This placement not only provided a basis for programming for the patients, but also enhanced the camp life for the established camper. It took them out of a competitive program in which they were previously forced because of numbers. The elder group was scheduled for trampoline, boating, archery, horseshoes, boccie, folk dance, basketball shooting, bowling, bean bag games, and frisbee golf which are relatively active sports. Large segments of time, however, were devoted to arts and crafts, cards, beano, checkers, music and just plain socializing. The original apprehension was not warranted as the aged turned out to be the most popular group in camp. Many of our staff and volunteers have become regular visitors to the nursing homes since the close of camp.

Those communities or organizations who are interested in implementing such a program in their community should consider possible aid and/or regulations from their state department of special education. The guidelines in Massachusetts include location, equipment, supplies, schedule, personnel qualifications, and enrollment. A program approved by the department of special education will be reimbursed for half of all expenditures made pertaining to the camp operation. This department also encourages all communities to participate so that greater numbers of retarded and handicapped people will be served. If a community cannot afford to begin a program on their own they encourage regionalization with many communities sharing the cost. The requirement that the department stresses most is concerned with the qualifications of staff. Well-qualified leadership is essential for a quality program. The director of a program for the mentally retarded must be a certified special education teacher. As far as enrollees, the department dictates the camp should be for those persons who cannot or should not participate in regular recreational programs. Complete daily attendance forms are kept on each individual person attending and a progress report carefully recorded. Finally, the recreation program must meet all demands of public health and safety requirements.

In budgeting a camp such as Happy Acres Day Camp, approximately 75 percent of all expenditures go directly into personnel. Other items included in the budget are a car allowance for the director, bus transportation for campers, milk, and the acquisition of supplies and equipment. As is the case in most communities, we have a very limited budget, therefore, leaders must keep an accurate inventory of the equipment issued to them and use a large degree of creativity in planning activities, especially arts and crafts. Several industries in the area have been very helpful to our camp by donating scrap materials such as leather goods, yarn and paper. I do not feel that an excessive budget is a prerequisite for a good camp, and Happy Acres Day Camp is a case in point. The key to running a good day camp is your staff, paid and unpaid, and the enthusiasm and competence they express in performing their duties. Given a suitable facility, a well-selected and trained staff and an adequate budget, any community or organization can begin and successfully operate a day camp for retarded children in their area.

SECTION III
THE EMOTIONALLY AND SOCIALLY MALADJUSTED

Walpole State Prison
Courtesy of Massachusetts Council on Crime and Correction, Inc.

Courtesy of Massachusetts Correctional Institution, Bridgewater, Massachusetts

CHAPTER 6

TAILORING RECREATION TO THE INDIVIDUAL IN A STATE PSYCHIATRIC HOSPITAL

Stephen M. Killourhy

IN ORDER TO SET UP a recreation program, the recreational therapist must be aware of the multifaceted differences between patients in the institution. Some of these differences developed as changes occurred within the field of mental health. Other differences are obviously created by the diverse individual emotional problems and symptoms affecting the patients. All of these differences must be taken into account if each individual is to be given the opportunity to benefit from the recreation program.

Major Changes in Mental Health

Three events in the 1960's resulted in major changes in the care and treatment given the emotionally disturbed by the states. The first and most pronounced was the publishing of the report of the Joint Commission of Mental Illness and Health, entitled *Action for Mental Health*. The Commission recommended that the large institutions (greater than 1000 beds) be closed because they were no longer the most effective way of treating patients. One of the major factors minimizing the effectiveness of the large institutions has been the use of drugs. Although drugs have not proven to be the cure-all that was initially hoped, therapists have been able to accomplish more with the medicated patient than had previously been possible when fewer means were available to curb the antisocial behavior of the patient. As a result, the patient's average length of stay in the hospital has been greatly shortened, and consequently the Commission felt that the funds used to maintain half-filled hospitals could be curtailed and put to better use within the mental health field. Eventually, these large institutions are to be replaced by day and evening care clinics, nursing homes, crisis prevention centers, and other small facilities set up for short-term comprehensive treatment. The communities, in conjunction with the state, will be responsible for providing therapy for individuals from their geographic area. State hospitals are therefore adapting their facilities to meet these future plans by setting up what is known as the unit system. Incoming patients are sent to wards in the hospital which represent their towns of residence, and there they are diagnosed, treated, and eventually released either on their own or to one of the community facilities.

The second event was the passage of Medicaid legislation. Some patients, who had been cured of their emotional illness many years before Medicaid, had remained wards of the state because their families were unwilling or unable to provide financial support for a nursing home or supervised care at home. With Medicaid funds, these patients now have the opportunity to go to nursing homes.

The third factor in bringing about change in the field of mental health was the emphasis on the civil rights of the individual which reached its peak in the 1960's. Legislation was passed which was originally meant to cover ethnic minorities, but which was extended to include all groups from prison inmates to the handicapped. As a result, commitment procedures were rewritten. Previously, commitment of a person to a psychiatric institution could be easily arranged by a member of the family and a consenting physician, and the length of stay depended upon the resident doctors attending the patient. Now, except in cases referred to the hospital by the courts or patients who enter and stay on a voluntary basis, the patient is initially committed for a six-month period, and then his case must be reviewed annually. The individual has a right to a hearing before a judge at which he is represented by a member of a legal aid society. In order to prevent the patient's leaving the institution, the hospital must prove that the individual is not ready to be released.

As a result of these three changes, persons who are capable of functioning with minimal supervision are sent to limited care centers where they can integrate back into society when ready without having to enter an institution. The patient population within a psychiatric institution at the present time is divided into two distinct groups. One is the newly admitted patients whose stay will average six months or less; the second group includes the chronic patients who have been institutionalized for many years and who need extended treatment due to the long-term effects of hospitalization in a custodial setting. Recreation will have to offer two separate programs to these groups.

Recreation for Newly Admitted Patients

Activities for the newly admitted patients with privileges to leave the ward are the easiest to provide. Usually, these patients can organize themselves, given some supervision. Volunteers enjoy working with them because the patients can participate with a minimum amount of instruction and variation of the game equipment and rules. Such activities as volleyball, tennis, softball, and basketball can be conducted as friendly games or include more competitive elements as in an intramural program or with games involving outside groups. Team sports can help establish a group identity. Even those who are not active in the events themselves can be involved with other important aspects, such as scoring, setting up equipment, or being active spectators.

Newly admitted patients who have limited privileges need the most active programs because of the amount of free time they have available. Since these activities must be conducted on the ward where a minimal amount of space is available, the recreational therapist has limited alternatives in setting up activities. The type of activities can be placed in two categories. The first type should be simple due to the limited attention span of many newly admitted patients, but intense because these patients are usually restless. Exercise programs are quite effective as well as dances or parties held on the ward. The second type should be games which can be easily learned. Once these have been set up and taught to one group, they can usually be carried over from one group to the next.

Recreation for Chronic Patients

The recreational therapist spends the maximum time in sponsoring activities for the chronic patients. Due to their limited skills, activities must be kept simple, yet diversified to prevent boredom. Here the therapist must use his imagination. He must effectively teach the basic skills needed in various activities and then develop a program in which these skills are used. Once the chronic patient has developed coordination, skills of throwing, kicking, and catching, other people will be more interested in working with him and including him in activities.

Recreation for Specific Psychiatric Disorders

Although basically geared to individual capabilities, a recreational program should also consider the particular disorder of the person. Emotional disorders may be divided into three areas: (1) neurotic, which are disorders of the nervous system, (2) psychotic, which are characterized by mental aberrations and delusions, and (3) drug-related, including alcoholism. In order to provide an effective program, the therapist must have a general knowledge of these disorders, their symptoms and the patient's emotional needs as characterized by this disorder.

Neurotic

A person with a nervous problem will exhibit excessive fear and anxiety. He may not be able to sleep at night and may have muscular twiches. He will often require close attention and may attempt futile plans. Some neurotics have a transient personality, that is, they are capable of functioning with no problems until placed in a specific situation which creates extreme anxiety. This fear is directed to specific situations such as being confined to an area which may cause claustrophobia. In this instance, the purpose of the recreation program is to aid in alleviating the effects of situational stress. This may be accomplished by almost any type of exercise of a nature which is interesting to the patient, suited to his physical tolerance, and favorable to the environmental readjustments desired. The therapist should attempt to handle the patient in an objective manner, trying to remove any baseless fear. Psychoneurotics will show overt hostile or overt affectionate behavior. Attempts should be directed toward aiding in the relief of the anxiety. This should involve exercise and play activities requiring exaggerated movement, with the desired result being the externalizing of the anxiety into activity. The recreational therapist's manner here must be firm. For both the transient personality and the psychoneurotic, the pleasure of the action resulting from the vocal and physical removal of stress should be emphasized rather than the activity itself, since the patient has a tendency to do everything to extremes. At times, the problem may be increased by the fact that the individual has replaced the anxiety with defense mechanisms which make it more difficult to reach him.

Psychotic

Psychotics are of two types, schizophrenic and manic depressive. Schizophrenics have become commonly known as "split personalities." The schizophrenic is extremely insecure in his relationships with others and very sensitive to everything that happens around him. Being unable to express his feelings, he keeps everything in, becoming resentful and withdrawn. However, he tries to show none of these feelings to those around him. The schizophrenic respects power, and all relationships become a struggle for control, making it difficult to work with the schizophrenic. He responds to advice and pressure by withdrawing and to permissiveness by inertia, that is, by having no response. The future of the individual lies in breaking through the autistic barriers. A friendly atmosphere must be established to attract the patient into social relationships. Often, this is done most easily by developing his known or inherent skills, and avoiding criticism of his efforts. It is also necessary to refrain from competition and pressure. He must learn to participate for his own satisfaction, not just to please others. Activities that can build his ego, such as weight-lifting, are good.

The manic depressive state is divided into two phases. During the depressed stage, the individual is unable to enjoy life because he feels unworthy. He will try to isolate himself and inflict other forms of self-punishment. The therapist can provide activities which are not self-destructive but which serve to remove the guilt feelings. Such projects as cleaning bowling balls or doing exercises which require repetition before they become tiring are good ways to provide relief from guilt feelings. In conjunction with this, the therapist should avoid sympathy and maintain an attitude of detached kindness. The manic cycle is the exact opposite of the depressed stage. The individual will be an extrovert, trying all activities, seldom completing any of them. He needs immediate gratifications and cannot restrain impulses. If possible, a one-to-one relationship is best because he requires the undivided attention of the people around him and is therefore disruptive in group activities. He is also likely to become overstimulated by trying to do what everyone else is doing. Any activity requiring constant movement which will eventually tire the patient will help in bringing him down. The therapist should be careful to avoid overexertion because the individual will do anything to extremes during the manic phase.

Unless the social relationships and activities of the psychotic patient can be altered, then all other forms of therapy will not be enough to rehabilitate him. He must find acceptable ways of releasing his pent-up emotions in order to stay mentally healthy.

Drug-Related

Drug-related patients may have one or more of the above disorders and use drugs as an escape mechanism. The first problem of the therapist involves rebulding the individual physically since his arrival at the hospital is frequently accompanied by malnutrition. Then he may go on to one of the prescribed therapies recommended by the psychiatrist in his diagnosis.

General Guidelines

While directing his program toward the different needs and capabilities of the patients, the recreational therapist should remember that some guidelines should apply to all. First, participation should be kept voluntary, except in a few cases recommended by the doctor. The quickest way to create dislike for an activity and for the therapist is to force an individual to participate. Second, the recreational therapist should set up a schedule and try to follow it. If people are expecting an activity, they may be frustrated and disappointed if the activity is cancelled. The staff is there to help, and if the patient loses confidence in the staff, then treatment will be even more difficult. Third, activities and the level and intensity at which they are conducted should be carefully watched. Excessive physical competition should be avoided. The purpose of the program is to develop confidence, not to make a patient more insecure. The therapist should also prevent patients from undertaking projects which will result in continually frustrating experiences. If help is required, the therapist should give supportive assistance to insure the success of the activity and not perform the activity for the patient. Activities should be curtailed at their peak. This will help to promote continued interest in the program. Fourth, patients should be given the opportunity to participate in activities which will take them away from their daily surroundings. This increases enthusiasm for the activity and for recreation in general. Fifth, activities which require cooperation and socialization are important. Too often patients isolate themselves, and social activities should help to draw them out.

Recreational therapy is designed to bring about social adjustment. The skills taught and the individual proficiency developed are of secondary importance. Primarily the recreational therapist is concerned with the physical, social, mental, and emotional well-being which these skills help to produce. Recreation can lessen tension, increase perceptual awareness, and improve socialization and interaction. But, in order to produce any of these results, the recreational therapist must be aware that the focus of his program is always the individual.

BIBLIOGRAPHY

Davis, John Eisile: *Clinical Application of Recreational Therapy*. Springfield, Illinois, Charles C Thomas, 1952.

Joint Commisstion on Mental Illness and Health, Final Report: *Action for Mental Health*. New York, Basic Books, Inc., 1961.

Rathbone, Josephine L., and Lucas, Carol: *Recreation in Total Rehabilitation*. Springfield, Illinois, Charles C Thomas, 1959.

CHAPTER 7

DOING TIME—THE PRISON SCENE

Frank M. Robinson, Jr.

Introduction

"Doing time" is the notorious byword of inmates who are incarcerated in prison systems throughout the world. It typically expresses the futility of a way of life offering little hope or fulfillment. Time is killed, wasted or eliminated from a calendar marking the ultimate day of release. This paper is concerned with that portion of time in which the inmate is free of commitments or obligations—it is his time to use. This spare or leisure time is particularly vital to the incarcerated individual because it can become debilitating. Spent creatively it will bring satisfactions, fulfillment and a sense of personal worth which support the very foundations of rehabilitation. Recreation is synonymous with the positive use of leisure time and contains the ingredients of social acceptability, freedom of choice and enjoyment. Herein lies a dilemma. What socially acceptable opportunities can exist for the offender if he lives in fear and danger? What voluntary choices are available for the prisoner whose life is regimented and influenced by the pressures of both inmates and guards? What enjoyment prospects are possible in a closed community? Lastly, what are the prevalent attitudes of prison officials toward recreation and can they be changed?

Clemmer, in his book, *The Prison Community*, states, "although the attitudes of prisons toward spare time are of importance, the prison environment prohibits the development of a pleasurable state of mind which persons in the free community experience."[1] This statement infers that a pleasurable state of

---

1. Donald Clemmer, *The Prison Community*. New York, Holt, Rinehart and Winston, 1968, p. 273.

mind is a necessary ingredient of recreation, that it is experienced by free men, but is not possible within the prison environment. It is difficult to refute this difference and yet I question this truth in its entirety. We recognize that walls, cells and guards prevent the very freedom that allows for a pleasurable state of mind to exist. It is also obvious that the voluntary aspect of recreation which encourages free choice greatly influences the satisfactions derived from it. We cannot, however, be so naive as to think that people outside of prison are totally happy or free of constraints and restrictions. Economic controls, laws, age restraints, physical, mental, and social limitations as well as time factors frequently thwart all of us from participating in some of our most treasured leisure pursuits. To some extent we all live within certain boundaries. The disabled person confined to a wheelchair has very few opportunities to pursue the leisure time activity of his choosing. The nature of his handicap and societal barriers drastically reduce his options, and yet a majority of disabled people are able to adjust and to achieve satisfactions during leisure despite existing conditions.

The real comparative difference is one of attitude and in the degree to which a community is therapeutic. It is not the constraints so much that affect us, but the extent of supportive assistance which can be delivered to those in need. If this rationale has any validity, then recreation with disciplinary controls is possible even within prison walls if the environment is generally receptive. Such a climate would help to make time live and change the "doing time" syndrome to a more positive "making time count."

A Time Analysis

Does the time schedule of the inmate differ from the man on the street? Perhaps looking at an in-depth study will reveal some comparative insights into this question.

One of the most detailed analyses of leisure, with its social and economic implications is the Southern California study. A similar type of study has not been found on the inmate population, so this segment of the analysis is estimated from discussions with a number of prison officials throughout the state of Massachusetts.

Time-Use Study	Percent for All Groups[2]	Percent for Prison Inmates[3]
Sleeping, eating, and personal care	47	46
Leisure	25	32
Work and related travel	12	18
Housework and child care (housekeeping)	9	1
School and study	5	2
Other unpaid productive activities (chores)	2	1

Each of these categories for the general population varies greatly according to the age, sex or social role of the individual. For instance, the school and study category would obviously be much higher for school-age youth and much lower for older people. Whereas employed Southern Californians were found to work 40.5 hours each week for pay, the young, the old, the unemployed, vacations and holidays reduce this figure to the 12 percent or 20 hours per week. The Southern California Research Council summarizes the way in which this free time appears:

> Leisure is taken in bits and pieces. According to our time budget for Southern California, about one third of all leisure hours is taken as daily leisure, in small pieces after school or work. About one fourth is absorbed by family members and in weekend pursuits. Vacations and holidays are the settings for yet another one sixth of the total. The remaining one fourth is time spent "at leisure" by children too young for school, retired persons, the chronically unemployed and the institutional populations.[4]

Since we are, in effect, comparing the entire populations within this geographic area, including those within penal institutions, to a specifically inmate population, these two comparisons become even more closely aligned. It is interesting to note in this study that leisure occupies between 50 to 70 hours per week for the young and the old and between 25 to 30 hours per week for most adults. The incarcerated adult has comparatively 54 hours of leisure each week. These hours become long ones indeed with no purchasing power. While the leisure boom has "set off an explosion of recreational spending in the United States estimated

---

2. Richard Kraus, *Recreation and Leisure in Modern Society*. New York, Appleton-Century-Crofts, 1971, p. 313.
3. Interviews with prison officials.
4. Kraus, *Op. Cit.*, p. 314.

at $105 billion in 1972,"[5] commercial recreation opportunities are almost nonexistent in our prisons. The offender's time use is almost totally dependent on his own initiative and the provisions available to him.

Educationally you have subgroups within the prison. One group gets involved with educational release programs, high school equivalency courses, correspondence courses or basic adult education. Another subgroup is basically unmotivated to better themselves through schooling opportunities.

In reflecting on the comparison of 42 hours of leisure per week for the general population as opposed to 54 hours of spare time for the inmate population certain questions come to mind.

Which group . . .
>is educationally prepared in leisure skills?
>has opportunities to learn leisure skills?
>has the purchasing power for commercial recreation?
>utilizes natural resources and other areas and facilities during leisure?
>has qualified leadership for leisure?
>appropriates an adequate budget for organized recreation?
>has occasion to join organization or hobby groups?
>has positive social relationship opportunities?
>has the opportunity to contribute to others during leisure?
>takes advantage of family recreation?
>can spend leisure hours at a secondary job?

In each of these categories and many others, the inmate group has far less or no opportunity at all while consuming 2808 spare hours per year in other less acceptable ways.

Could work programs be increased to turn some of these leisure hours into work hours? Since work is the third largest time-use category, it is important to learn what is happening to work in our prisons.

The Demise of Prison Industry

Work has taken many forms within our prison systems from the antiquated forced labor version to the modern ideal of voca-

---
5. Leisure boom: Biggest ever and still growing, *U. S. News and World Report*, Vol. LXXII, No. 16, April 17, 1972, p. 42.

tional preparation. Through the years prison industry has been a major occupier of the time gap. Long hours of work at least gave the offender something to do, perhaps some sense of accomplishment, and it tired the inmate physically so he slept well and was more easily controlled. Work is still viewed traditionally by many people as the only door to salvation, the only way the convict can make restitution for his sins.

A brief recapitulation of the systems of prison labor in our country will provide some insight on what has happened in prison industry and where it is going.

Systems of Prison Labor

The "lease system" which became popular during the Civil War era turned convicts over to a private leasee who not only worked them, but also fed, clothed, guarded, housed and disciplined them. In effect, the health, morality and other considerations of a convict's welfare became neglected and a form of semi-slavery developed. Scandals, growing out of its abuse, led to abandonment of the lease system in the United States. This was gradually supplanted by the so-called piece-price variety of a "contract system" where the contractor supplied the raw materials and agreed to pay for the product of the prisoners' labor at a stipulated price per piece. This system eliminated private control of prisoners, but difficulties developed between contractors and their methods of marketing. As a result, the "public account system" was introduced where the State bought the raw material, assumed all risk of conducting a manufacturing business, and state agents sold the product on the public market. Labor organizations violently opposed this practice and it was branded as unfair competition undercutting private enterprise. Free labor demanded a cessation of both the "contract" and "public account systems." Where labor organizations were strong, they either abolished practically all prison labor or forced states to adopt the "state use system." It is interesting to note that convict labor, despite labor union claims, has never been a serious competitor with free labor in American Industry. In 1905 convict labor produced less than one quarter of 1 percent of the total goods manufactured. In the "state use system" prison-made products can not compete on the free market and the sale of goods is limited to state institutions for their own consumption. "The Hawes-Cooper Act of 1929 and the Ashurst-Summers Act of 1934 limited the sale of prison goods on the open market and culminated in the Act of 1941 which forbade their shipment in interstate commerce. These laws produced a serious idleness in Penal Institutions."[6] Prison industries boomed temporarily during the World War II period as morale improved when prisoners could share in the war effort. Today the "state use system" is still the most prevalent and generally approved practice of prison industries, yet, it continues to cause some drastic problems. The reduction of work causes a lack of motivation resulting in inefficiency and inferior goods. Many shops became overstaffed and a scandalous amount of idleness prevails among the inmates which is a chief cause of demoralization and prison riots.

A variant of the "state use system" is the "public works and ways system" also in practice today. Included here is road construction, reforestation, prevention of soil erosion, agricultural labor and other forms of outdoor work. Prison farm work is recommended for selected men for its vocational advantage to those going into farming and as a health and therapeutic aid. The "public works and ways system" must select work that is useful yet not commercially profitable or construction companies will oppose it.

Some inroads have been made toward instituting compensation or wages for prisoners but it is basically a meager sum. In Massachusetts inmates at Walpole, Norfolk, Concord and Framingham Correctional Institutions are paid for work at the rate of 25 to 50 cents a day. The specialized industry allocated to these four state prisons are as follows:

Walpole—brushes, foundry products, cast iron man-hole frames and covers, roadside markers, printing items.

Norfolk—cotton clothing, concrete lawn furniture, cemetery

---

6. Donald Taft and Ralph England, *Criminology*. New York, The Macmillan Co., 1971, p. 453.

markers, park benches, mattresses and pillows, galvanized pails, men and women's shoes.

Concord—reinforced concrete pipe and wooden furniture.

Framingham (women)—towels, hospital supplies, flags and banners, sheets and bedspreads.[7]

This job experience has very little vocational use to prisoners upon their release. How much opportunity is there for employment of an ex-con with an occupational history of making manhole covers? Since most of these products are in demand only by the State and subdivisions of it, the released offender has no free market employment skills or background from which to make a new start. The first inmate who tries to benefit on the outside from his inside license plate experience will be thrown back in the jug without delay.

Trends and Problems

The most notorious and significant defect in American prison industry is the fact that it has made almost no provision for the teaching of a trade to convicts so that they can make an honest living after discharge. The official report of the President's Commission on Law Enforcement and Administration of Justice, the report of Manpower and Training in Correctional Institutions and other publications make some interesting points from which change must evolve. Some of the ideas are already being tried, such as wage payments and other incentives. Rhode Island permits deduction of sentences two days per month for satisfactory work. "Other proposals, such as choice of employment in line with vocational aptitude, assurance of assistance in securing a job after release, fair promotion practices and diplomas indicating job skills and accomplishments are not widespread practices."[8]

Work release programs are on the upswing where inmates work outside the walls in private employment. The record is generally favorable in Massachusetts although the small percentage of failures are attracted to newspaper headlines.

---

7. Interview with Mr. O'Laughlin, Massachusetts Department of Corrections.

8. The President's Commission on Law Enforcement and the Administration of Justice, *The Challenge of Crime in a Free Society*. New York, Avon Books, 1968, p. 397.

In Massachusetts, the Sheriff can establish a work-release or study-release program in his house of correction. Sentenced prisoners (except sex offenders) can leave the institution to work in private employment or connected educational training. His pay goes through the Sheriff and is alloted to the releasee for travel and expenses, a portion to support his family, a percentage to public welfare and to the prisoner upon release. This program is not new as Superintendent Miriam Van Waters of the Massachusetts Reformatory for Women in Framingham established it for many years after 1910; it is, however, common in Europe today and becoming more prevalent in the United States.

Whatever the solution to our prison industry problems, relying on the "state use system" isn't enough and strong measures must be taken to provide a modern day system which will lead to a rehabilitated individual. Work can help to fill that important time void in a constructive way, but changes must be realized. A Correction Industries Commission has been set up in California with labor, industry, agriculture and the general public represented. This appears to be a thrust in the right direction.

Lack of an industrial market has sharply reduced work within the prison to the point that much inmate time assigned to workgangs or the shop is actually spent loafing. This gives education, spiritual guidance and recreation the additional responsibility of providing positive input to this time-gap.

Forced Loitering or Re-Creation

According to Webster, to loiter is to linger along a way, to hang about and to waste time. Loitering is also a form of idleness frequently leading to antisocial acts which are destructive and injurious to self or performed against society at large. Forced loitering is negative and in total opposition to re-creation which is the positive, creative and constructive use of time. Are we forcing our people who are confined in prison to loiter because of insufficient provision for educational, recreational, spiritual and vocational opportunities? The idleness that was ever-present two years ago at Attica provided the fuel which launched one of the most tragic episodes in prison history.

> The prisoners at Attica wanted better food . . .
> more pay for their work in the prison shops . . .
> lower prices in the commissary . . .
> more freedom to act politically . . .
> more freedom to practice religion . . .
> more recreation . . .
> no censorship of letters or magazines . .
> more liberal communication with the outside world . . .
> expansion of day jobs outside . . .
> better treatment by guards . . .
> better training of guards to handle Attica's problems . . .
> home leaves for some prisoners . . .
> removal of the prison superintendent . . .
> total amnesty for all who participated in the riot.[9]

The latter two were the only wants not recognized by the authorities as being legitimate requests.

A Leisure Profile

Studies point out that the majority of prisoners are lacking an educational background and are deficient in recreational skills, interests and experiences. When a group has few supportive resources the need for a more highly regulated and organized program becomes vital. This requires initially strong leadership and instruction to organize, to teach skills and to prepare the group for less structured activity. Clemmer reports that only 4 percent of the total leisure time block within prisons is regulated or organized and that the much larger portion is unregulated activity. So much unregulated time leads to gambling, drug use, escape plans, con games, rioting and general discontent within the walls. If the inmate cannot create something useful to do in his spare time and be given the support to carry it through, he then becomes a victim of his spare time. He will be the victim of boredom, nothingness and his own weaknesses or ultimately succumb to the vultures who prey on idlers.

In most prisons recreation is considered as basically a physical activity for emotional and physical energy release. Baseball, basketball, football and soccer games, boxing matches and other

---

9. Richard, Ray: Politics, trips home, pay among inmate demands. *Boston Globe*, Sept. 14, 1971, p. 24.

sporting events usually dominate the overall program offerings. This helps to meet the needs of the athletically inclined, but not the majority. The entire social, cultural and mental areas are frequently neglected. Most prisons officially sponsor movies and letter writing, reading, radio listening, visits, group meetings and clubs take up some of the time slack, however, it falls far short of meeting the need.

The Recreation Director in many prisons is unqualified for the position. Frequently his primary job is as a guard while recreation is only a secondary responsibility. How much can be expected of a person in this situation?

Many prisoners with their low educational background and inadequate vocational preparation will, when released, be qualified only for routine jobs or operating a machine. These dull and unchallenging jobs leave little chance to gain personal satisfactions from work; satisfactions will have to come during leisure. When will correctional institutions begin to adequately prepare inmates to use their large blocks of leisure time wisely so that positive satisfactions can be gained now and in the future? This point is emphasized by Clemmer's statement "the greatest single obligation of a prison is to stimulate and provide interests of a wholesome nature in spare time activities."[10]

Can they be stimulated? When, how and by whom?

Attitudes and Priorities

Penal institutions which are in name "correctional" have many difficulties to overcome before they can effectively prescribe treatment which will correct the social disorder of the offender. The cause of the crime must be accurately diagnosed before a treatment program can be prescribed. Does a man forge a bank check because he is insecure, lazy, he lacks excitement, he dislikes work, he has a psychological hang-up, he has no skills to make an honest living or because he thinks the world owes him a living? If the cause is diagnosed then how can the behavior pattern of the convicted criminal be changed? Changing the attitudes and behavior of people is a tremendous undertaking. It requires highly moti-

---

10. Clemmer, *op. cit.,* p. 276.

vated and creative people who really care. With professional preparation and large scale financial backing a rehabilitation team has a good chance to redirect the "revolving door syndrome, where 70 percent of those prisoners released return to prison within two years."[11] They must, however, obtain public support. Attitude change is not impossible, because after all, wasn't the old idea that criminals were "possessed by devils" altered gradually to the modern attitude that convicts have a "psychological disability"? But will the public support and pay for rehabilitative programs to the extent that they are needed? With austerity constantly staring us in the face and health, education, welfare and other more acceptable social programs feeling the pinch, what priority expectations are possible for our penal system?

To propose a comprehensive fully funded therapeutic recreation program in the prisons at the expense of health or educational needs on the outside would be suicidal. Even if the social needs of the public are sufficiently funded, the attitude and response would still be—what are you promoting, a country club? Why should we be teaching recreational skills and granting recreational privileges? Won't more crimes be committed just to be readmitted to such an institution?

Attitude and behavioral change plus a reordering of priorities by the general public will be long coming. Meanwhile "the private citizen is paying 8000 dollars per year to maintain one inmate in our failing prisons."[12]

What percentage of this cost is for rehabilitation? Rather than wait for money and acceptance, recreation professionals can initiate positive action, particularly in short term institutions for minor offenders.

A Proposal

A therapeutic recreation program within the Correctional Institution should be developed in cooperation with its immediate and adjacent communities as well as utilizing the vast resources of society at large. Since many municipal departments are ill pre-

---

11. Archdiocesan Commission on Penal Reform. *A Guide for Community Action in Penal Reform.* Boston, Paulist Center Committee for Correctional Reform, June, 1973, p. 18.

12. Ibid, p. 11.

pared to initiate such programs independently, I propose that Departments of Recreation within Colleges and Universities carry the ball. Such an experience will provide a realistic challenge to students in an unfamiliar laboratory; it will help to pave the way for community involvement and demonstrate to prison officials and inmates that someone cares and is willing to try. It is vital to select a mature student to administer the program. He must be suited to work with the inmate population and strongly supported by both the university and the community. If Federal or state funding is not available to underwrite the project, the student administrator's salary should be obtained from private sources.

Rationale and Goals

Recreation is vitally important in the rehabilitative setting because it can help to offset a lack of opportunity to find satisfaction through work and family. If the prisoner is expected to improve or at least not degenerate while "doing time" in prison, his need for art, drama, sports, motors, reading, rock music, gardening and other leisure pursuits must be accommodated. While accepting and working within the realities of security measures, facility limitations, budget deprivations and atypical participants, a positive recreation program based in the correctional institution and community still has the potential to make rehabilitation really work. The role of recreation in the modern prison is just as essential as nourishing food, clean living quarters, productive labor and sound counseling. Goals are:

1. To develop the nucleus of a strong functional recreation program to meet the needs of inmates.
2. To stimulate the inmate to participate in these leisure time pursuits for his personal satisfaction.
3. To train selected inmates to assist in conducting the program.
4. To combat idleness and relieve pressure within the prison.
5. To encourage community responsibility through involvement and participation.
6. To provide selected upper-class students with a valuable experience.

Organization and Procedures

An *ad hoc* planning committee will serve in an advisory capacity and guide the project to its goals. This committee will consist of six members; one representative of the inmates being trained, a prison official or recreation director at the prison, the recreation director within the community, a citizen at large, the project coordinator (professor) and project administrator (graduate student).

A small team of students will assist the project administrator and coordinator in training five to eight selected inmates in leadership techniques and activity skills. These trainees will play a major role in conducting the program and in strengthening relationships and responsibility among the inmates for the program. Administrative procedures are briefly:

1. Recruit inmate trainee staff.
2. Inventory existing facilities and programs within the prison and in surrounding communities.
3. Assess recreational needs of the inmates (questionnaire and interview).
4. Design a functional training institute for inmate staff geared to inmate needs.
5. Design a realistic program both on the inside and outside communities.
6. Develop evaluative criteria to measure results.

Schedule

The project is designed for 26 weeks with the project administrator working at least 20 hours per week on site. Other students as well as interested local groups, such as church and Jaycees, contribute time and resources.

Weeks 1 through 3 will be spent assessing facilities, determining needs, designing the program and training institute.

Weeks 4 through 6 will be devoted to working with the inmates who are selected as trainees.

Weeks 7 through 10 will involve two hours of training and four hours of conducting the program each week.

Weeks 11 through 25 will be spent in program both at the prison and in the community.

Week 26—evaluation of the training institute and the total program.

This proposal is limited in scope, but it represents a start. The six-month time span is selected to coincide with the average length of sentence at the prison. It also conforms to the quarter schedule for Northeastern University students.

A county or minimum security prison is recommended because chances of implementing the programs are greater, there is less danger, goals can be more easily achieved and the opportunity for community involvement is better.

Unless people and communities become actively concerned we are just fooling ourselves by advocating that penal institutions are correctional. They can only rehabilitate if we the people become involved enough to see that it actually happens. If given the chance, therapeutic recreation programs which build responsibility and channel drives and interests into positive uses of time will play a vital role toward achieving rehabilitative ends.

BIBLIOGRAPHY

Allan, Barbara, Doing My Time on the Outside, *Fortune News,* New York, The Fortune Society, May, 1973.

Archiocesan Commission on Penal Reform: *A Guide for Community Action in Penal Reform.* Boston, Paulist Center Committee for Correctional Reform, June 1973.

Clemmer, Donald: *The Prison Community.* New York, Holt, Rinehart and Winston, 1968.

Curtis, Joseph E., A Proposal to Provide Improved Recreation and Physical Fitness Opportunities for Inmates of Massachusetts Correctional Institutions. March, 1973.

Decker, E. Larry: Recreation in Correctional Institutions, *Parks and Recreation,* April, 1969.

Kraus, Richard: *Recreation and Leisure in Modern Society.* New York, Appleton-Century-Crofts, 1971.

Leisure boom: Biggest ever and still growing. *U.S. News and World Report,* Vol. LXXII, No. 16, April, 1972.

President's Commission on Law Enforcement and the Administration of Justice: *The Challenge of Crime in a Free Society.* New York, Avon Books, 1968.

Richard, Ray: Politics, trips home, pay among inmate demands. *Boston Globe,* September 14, 1971.

Shafer, Stephen: *Theories in Criminology.* New York, Random House, 1969.

Stump, George: *Treating the Untreatable.* Baltimore, Johns Hopkins Press, 1968.

Taft, Donald and England, Ralph: *Criminology.* New York, Macmillan, 1971.

SECTION IV

THE ELDERLY

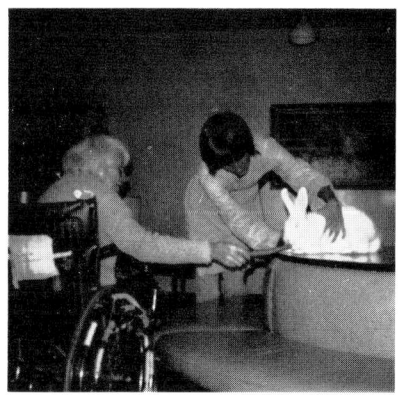

Courtesy of Thera-Care, Inc.
Brookline, Massachusetts

Courtesy of Cliff House
Nursing Home
Winthrop, Massachusetts

CHAPTER 8

THE ROLE OF THE RECREATION THERAPIST IN THE LONG-TERM HEALTH CARE FACILITY

ELIZABETH C. ALLEN

IN ORDER TO ASSESS the value of recreation therapy in the long-term health care facility and to be able to cope with the problems and frustrations of planning and implementing recreation therapy programs in these facilities, it is necessary to understand the past, present and projected future roles for the facility itself and the key personnel staffing this facility.

For purposes of review the following dates are used:

Past—prior to Medicare
Present—1960 to 1980
Future—1980 onward

It must be understood that these dates are not static but continuous time periods separated only for purposes of gaining perspective.

Past

In the post-depression era of the thirties there were no nursing homes as we know them today. Those patients able to afford private care lived in rest homes which provided a quality of care from poor to excellent depending on the philosophy and business acumen of the operator. Public health regulations were virtually nonexistent and there was no programming for patient care. Those patients who could not afford private facilities were channelled to poor farms or state hospitals depending on the amount of medical care needed, with more people ending in state hospitals as the poor farms were phased out. Although many of the patients did not need psychiatric services at the time of their admission, endless years of unprogrammed care resulted in emotional problems needing eventual treatment. Because of the improvement in the welfare structure, nursing homes gradually took the place of state hospitals in providing care for the elderly.

With the increasing number of elderly persons needing supervised care after World War II, nursing homes became more numerous in the fifties, still fairly free of regulation and supervision, still understaffed with poorly trained personnel.

In the past health care providers in our nursing homes were primarily nurses and physicians. The physician was the key figure in the health care field, especially in the hospitals. All of the programming was structured around his personal presence and the professional code for all of the other health care personnel was very specific in outlining this relationship.

Because of his increased work load with the elderly and the limitations put on him by the reimbursement agencies, the physician was never the key figure in patient care in the nursing home as opposed to his role in the hospital. While he had to formulate a medical care plan for his patient, he depended on the nursing personnel to carry it out. Indeed, he often modified or changed his orders on the considered recommendation of a dependable director of nursing or supervisor.

Prior to 1970 the nurse in charge was the pivotal force in the nursing home, often assuming a multiplicity of roles and job responsibilities. She functioned as the social worker on an "as needed" basis, provided whatever recreation there was, supervised the kitchen and the laundry (if not actually supplying these services herself), taught her ancillary personnel, handled the business affairs of the facility, and very often worked a double shift on weekends. Like a devoted mother she worked endlessly with little recognition or tangible reward.

In the past the administrator, if there were one for the facility, functioned primarily as the business manager. Often the facility was run with an absentee administrator. Quite often the owner himself served in this capacity. He was budget-oriented and usually had no specific education in health care. There were no licensure requirements for him. Generally, he was not involved with either the program or the patient, except in a superficial way.

The patient was a nonentity for the most part, regimented, scheduled, bathed and fed. In most nursing homes he did not even dress for the day—there was no reason to. He was also silent and uncomplaining, quite often a social derelict grown accustomed to the progressive limitations to his freedom of choice and mobility as his finances dwindled. Most pitiful of all was his own awareness of his decreasing value as an individual. During his productive years he was oriented to a 72-hour work week with time off for some religious experience either by choice or habit and he had no concept of recreation or personal fulfillment as a realistic goal. His wife had much the same orientation except that by training she was arts and crafts-oriented.

Present

With the advent of the Medicare program with its "Conditions for Participation," it became necessary for the nursing home owners and administrators to evaluate the quality of care they were providing in order to qualify for reimbursement under the new regulations. The need to classify facilities by the level of care given was soon apparent and by the late 1960's the Public Health Department had sent proposed drafts of regulations out in the field for review and comment. The programming required for these new regulations was unwieldy in itself, and the existing nursing home staff was generally not qualified to implement it.

The nursing home image was poor, with the nursing home classified as a stepsister to the hospital and under constant pressure trying to comply with the new rules and regulations while under continuous assault from all sides. The facility was understaffed for the new demands made of it; however, although it was over-regulated and over-regimented, it began to be progress-oriented and generally worked hard to meet the regulatory requirements.

When the director of nurses received administrative assistance, her work load was lightened but she was placed in the position of working under the direction of an administrator who knew less about her job than she did. Within a short period of time her responsibility for guaranteeing an accurate diet for the patient was assumed by a dietician, a social worker was hired to deal with the patient's social problems, occupational therapists were available to direct the patient's recreation and in many homes clinical specialists were hired to teach nursing.

Busier than ever because of the increased paper work, the nurse still suffered serious feelings of loss similar to the empty-nest syndrome we all recognize as one fact of life for the middle-aged mother and homemaker who had always done everything for everybody. It was necessary then for the nurse to redefine her role in the light of the many specialities of health care which she could no longer govern. Although she realized that her "forty daylight hours" were regulated by law, she felt more had been taken from her than she deserved to lose.

Catch phrases like "total patient care concept" and "team approach" became part of everyone's vocabulary and the administrator soon became the key figure in the facility, and the one to direct all of the several new disciplines.

The administrator, quite often young and inexperienced, was faced with the burden of accepting many responsibilities and directing many disciplines about which he was not knowledgeable, while struggling to meet regulatory requirements with insufficient reimbursements. He had neither the time nor the energy to upgrade himself professionally beyond the fifteen hours of unstructured study program required by law. The present smorgasbord of health care education offered to administrators can only disenchant the dedicated and bewilder and frustrate those seeking a worthwhile career in the field.

Influenced by the emergence of the individualistic philosophy of the so-called hippies, the senior citizenry also began to assert its right to do its own thing and became highly vocal in crusading for equal rights for the elderly, freedom of choice, federal support, and a voice in the governing of its own affairs. Each group had its own militants. Whatever may be said against the volatile manner in which either of these groups programmed to reach its objectives, the objectives themselves began to be included in the philosophy for the health care of the institutionalized elderly to their advantage.

More and more we are admitting patients who read a great

deal, enjoy one or more hobbies, are used to some social involvement and expect to enjoy some form of recreation. These people cannot be expected to watch morning television in a spirit of passive acceptance.

The new rules and regulations are patient-oriented in concept and the nursing homes are required to staff and program to the regulatory requirements. One of these requirements is that some meaningful activity be provided for patients on a regularly scheduled basis by an employee specifically hired for this work. At the present time the qualifications state only that she have had a high school education, or the equivalent, and a year's leadership training, or the equivalent. The paucity of preparation in this area has already been recognized and a Federal law is now in effect that requires a specified amount of education in the therapeutic aspects of recreation for any employee providing recreation services for any patient in a Massachusetts nursing home.

Future Expectations

Within another ten years there will be no nursing homes, or hospitals as we know them today. I visualize two separate but equal health care facilities with the hospital offering intensive care and the nursing home offering extensive care. Let us define these terms for our understanding:

Intensive Care—compact, concise, to unite firmly as in a system, systematic

Extensive Care—expansive, to reach forth, to widen, to become larger or more comprehensive, diffuse, nonregimented

These disciplines will run in tandem with the nursing home equal and cooperative, although separate from the hospital, each having a vital part in the total health care program.

In the intensive care program there will be a centralization of those services dependent on expensive specific equipment and decentralization of those services dependent on fulfilling the social needs of the individual.

In the extensive care program there will be a centralization of those services requiring specific procedures and licensed supervision and a decentralization of those services dealing with human emotion and personal development.

The new extensive care facility of the future then will be a large complex offering four, five, six or more levels of health care services starting with the first plateau away from intensive care, i.e. skilled nursing care, and becoming less and less regimented (not less regulated) to provide more and more freedom of mobility and independent action for the patient. We can no longer expect to govern a person's life simply because we control his income any more than we can insist that a child live within the framework of what we feel is best for him simply because we are charged with the responsibility for his care.

The levels of care then would extend outward (not downward) from skilled care to supervisory, custodial, outpatient, supervised apartments, visiting health care services in all of the health disciplines, and adaptive housing for the elderly, if necessary, with temporary health services structured into each level. At all levels of care the emphasis would be on integrated living conditions for all of the consumers requiring that care, separating individuals neither by culture nor age. The only separative forces then would be the willingness to pay for a specific quality of environment within the facility or the availability of outside facilities for the fulfillment of certain personal needs such as education, recreation, and family involvement.

The less regimented the environment is for the patient the more expertise is needed to structure and control this environment within the framework of policy guidelines and regulatory requirements.

The physician servicing patients in the health care facility of the future will be required by regulation to devote more time to consultation, utilization reviews, and programming for total patient care. Although he will still be able to depend on the health care staff to carry out his orders, he will also have to delegate many of his routine examinations and procedures to a physician's assistant specifically trained for this responsibility. In addition to this, he will be involved with the training of health care practitioners to provide extended health care services under his direction.

The future administrator will be educated in the health care field through the master's degree level. The health care curriculum will include a survey course in all of the health care disciplines to provide a working knowledge of these and in-depth training in all areas of management and administration.

The nurse will also be different a decade from now. No longer will the nursing home provide a pasture for the aging nurse, too weary to become involved and too unfamiliar with the current concepts and procedures to be effective. Neither will it provide only temporary employment for the young nurse working while her husband obtains his education. Already the industry is attracting the young and vitally interested nurse. Ten years from now the director of nursing will have grown wiser, more comprehensive in her orientation to patient care and more professional in her methodology.

The patient also will be different ten years from now. He will have had more education, mobility and more opportunity for creative self-expression. He will be knowledgeable about the law and his rights under that law. He will have come to enjoy some form of relaxation and will expect that this need be satisfied. He will accept subsidy as a fact of life and will no longer be intimidated by his need of financial assistance. He will expect to have a voice in the governing of his own affairs. More and more he will also not be elderly. The phasing out of our state hospitals provides for many younger people the opportunity to live in a social environment conducive to self-realization. The use of mood control medications is opening doors to the possibility for these individuals to explore new vistas and create new life-styles. These patients will also be more alert because they will have greater opportunities for education which, simply defined, is only the opportunity to learn something today which one didn't know yesterday.

The possibilities in this area alone stagger the imagination, and more and more health care facilities are accepting the challenge and the frustration of working with the mentally indigent. Hopefully, also, there will be no institutionalized retardates who are potentially trainable or educable. To service all of these individuals will require very specific programming based on compassionate philosophies of patient care and extensive training and education in the health care disciplines. This should offer an exciting challenge for the re-creator interested in re-motivation or re-grooving techniques.

If you trace the professional evolvement of all of the primary health care providers in the long-term care facility, you will recognize the universal process of professional education which can be categorized at four levels: (1) learning through experience or apprenticeship; (2) learning from unstructured workshops and seminars; (3) learning from courses to meet certification or licensure requirements; and (4) learning through highly structured programs offered at the institutions for higher learning.

That recreation therapy has reached the fourth level of preparation at this time, while the Department of Health in Massachusetts is still requiring only level one preparation for recreation workers, is both a frustration and an opportunity.

To function as professionals in a field which does not recognize recreation as a therapy, or even understand the language in which we phrase our goals and objectives, is certainly frustrating; but to be part of a discipline which can lead the way for the professional advancement of the other restorative disciplines must surely make the commitment worthwhile.

CHAPTER 9

STARTING A RECREATION PROGRAM WITH LIMITED FUNDING IN NURSING HOMES

Linda Tracy Dudish

P ROVIDING RECREATION PROGRAMS for the aged who live in nursing homes is a relatively new idea. The need has been recognized by the increased number of elderly people who now live in these homes, and the belief that active involvement in later years has much therapeutic value. Recent government programs are attempting to upgrade conditions in nursing homes and thus improve patient care. Newly developed federal regulations now demand the availability of recreation programs in nursing homes.

The Concept of Recreation Therapy

Recreation therapy can create a new freshness in the lives of older people as well as enhance a desperately needed purpose for living. Webster defines recreation as "a restoration of refreshment in body and mind." Recreation can relieve loneliness, minimize boredom, and enrich the lives of the aged. Described in very simple terms, recreation can be a reason to get out of bed in the morning, something to plan for and anticipate.

When one woman of 72 years was asked what recreation meant to her, she replied—"something to keep me busy and a change of pace from the daily routine."

Another patient, a man of 65 years, stated that "recreation was having a good time."

Recreation can be referred to as the wise use of leisure. Undoubtedly elderly people are confronted with and must deal with large amounts of leisure time while in a nursing home. The hours can pass slowly or quickly depending on the amount of physical or mental activity. Through recreation therapy, the leisure of the aged can be utilized to develop social contacts, to be active in meaningful activities, and to gain feelings of purpose, usefulness and self-satisfaction. In essence, recreation can help to keep the aged happy, healthy and to maintain their identity.

Program Goals

The goals of an effective recreation therapy program for the elderly can include: (1) Restoration of self-care—the aged need to feel useful, secure, and independent: when possible to be able to make personal decisions, and to care for themselves. This self-care approach strengthens self-esteem and confidence. Recreation activities can encourage self-care duties and enhance autonomy. (2) Promotion and maintenance of normal living activities—recreation therapy can minimize the adjustment problems of living in a nursing home and being apart from friends, family and past living activities. Attaining a normal life in every aspect—physical, mental, and social—can be attempted through recreation. (3) Providing a happy, home-like environment—for many, a nursing home may be the only home that the aged know and a place where they will be spending their remaining years of life. It is important that they feel comfortable and a part of their new home. (4) Reaching each patient despite physical or mental disabilities—this goal involves diligent work and planning for the therapist, and offers a real professional challenge. Each patient must be viewed as being distinct, having an individual identity, and specific needs that can be reached by some type of planned activity.

The Functions of a Therapist

Having a genuine concern for the aged and their needs, the recreation therapist has an important and demanding role in the nursing home. Along with other members of the nursing home professional team, the recreation therapist attempts to provide a therapeutic community for these older persons.

The functions of a therapist are many and diverse. The chief one entails developing, planning, and initiating a wide range of meaningful activities for *all* patients. Because a range of capabilities among the aged exists, each patient must be considered individually. Before developing such a recreation program, each person should be personally interviewed to assess physical or mental handicaps, the participating potential of each, and, most important, individual interests and needs must be determined. The nursing staff may be able to relate their observations of patients and provide additional insight. After collecting such data, a recreation profile of each patient can be formed. These records will be basic to effective activity planning. Patients can then be grouped according to their capabilities and interests.

Motivating patient participation is another important function of the therapist. Posting a monthly activity calendar can be an effective means of stimulating patient interest and enthusiasm for planned activities. A well-planned program is useless without patient interest and cooperation. Being energetic and enthusiastic about a particular activity is crucial in getting your program "off the ground." Patients must accept recreation as a realistic goal. Growing up in a work-oriented society, the elderly often do not understand the concept of play. A man who has worked hard six days a week and spent the seventh day in church may have little understanding of what play means; he must be educated to this new concept. Patients should never be forced to participate in activities, because this could be psychologically damaging. Recreation is voluntary and some patients just may not be interested; it is their choice, and a therapist must recognize it and not get discouraged. Of the six daily living activities of the aged, which include rest, nutrition, personal hygiene, elimination, exercise, and recreation, the last activity is the only area in which the patients have any real choice to make personal decisions. To have a say in their own lives would be therapeutic.

Documenting patients' feelings, actions, and participation responses during recreation is still another function of the therapist. This record can describe who partakes in various activities, what specific activities have the greatest appeal among patients, and how the patients react to given situations. This record can be a means of noting the progress and behavioral responses of the patients.

Program Funding

Funding determines total patient care. The type of nursing home and the economic resources of its patients play an important role in the amount of available funds. If most patients are economically disadvantaged, a nursing home cannot afford many extras.

In a nursing home a hierarchy of priorities exist to promote good nursing care. Providing nutritious food for patients to eat, providing a clean, dry bed to sleep in, and administering prescribed medication on a regular basis are examples of top priorities. In addition to these, staff salaries must be paid and overall nursing home maintenance upheld. The expenses are numerous and costly. Recreation often has a low priority on the value scale. A budget to fund such recreation programs will be minimal because of these other essential priorities.

Despite curtailed recreation budgets, effective and stimulating programs are still very possible. Making the most of available resources is a challenging task for the therapist who must develop programs with limited funding. Bare-thread budget programming is being accomplished without fanfare in many nursing homes throughout the country.

The remaining portion of this chapter will deal with sample programs that require comparatively little money. They are beginning programs that have been introduced in homes where recreation is an entirely new concept.

LOW BUDGET BEGINNINGS
Crafts

Crafts are valuable recreation activities. Much happiness can be experienced "by doing." Making something that is tangible, that can be seen and admired, encourages feelings of personal accomplishments. Crafts involve developing simple skills and learning new things, thus promoting a mental challenge. Education is a lifelong process. The aged have a continuing capacity to learn, although they may learn at a slower pace.

In the beginning crafts program, start with simple projects that could interest a wide range of patients. Having basic art supplies available such as crayons, pencils, paints, scissors, paste, and paper, a therapist can initiate inexpensive craft projects. The following are ideas an arts and crafts program can include.

Collages

Photos from old magazines can be cut and pasted on large sheets of construction paper to make an attractive wall poster. Select a single theme and choose clippings that would depict it. Work with partners if necessary. A patient with use of only one hand, such as a stroke victim, may not be able to cut clippings but he can paste them.

Finger Painting

For those who find it difficult to hold a paint brush, such as a severe arthritic, try finger painting. A large roll of shelf paper can be bought cheaply and can make at least a dozen pictures. Moisten paper in water, dab a small amount of paint on the paper, and let your fingers, palm, forearm, and even elbow create an expressive painting.

Flower Vases

Save Michelob beer bottles. They can make colorful decoupage flower vases. Cut tiny pieces of bright tissue paper and paste them on the bottle in a mosaic pattern. Finish the bottle with a decoupage paste to give a lasting, glazed effect.

Necklaces

Believe it or not, sparkling necklaces can be made with only paper clips and contact paper. Link clips together in the shape of a dangling necklace. Add color by cutting snips of printed contact paper (preferably gold or silver) and surround each clip. The effects are amazing.

Party Decorations

Favors and decorations for holidays, seasons, and parties can be made with limited materials. Examples are paper Easter baskets, Spring tissue paper flowers, Christmas wreaths, and shamrocks.

Service Projects

Crocheting bandages for the Red Cross, making and stuffing pillows for the Children's Hospital at Christmas, or addressing and stamping envelopes for the Heart Association are examples of craft projects that can benefit the community and give patients a feeling of usefulness.

Arts and crafts as a therapy can rid patients of their frustrations. It allows them to organize their inner thoughts and to express feelings in a creative manner. A completed project can strengthen one's self-confidence and encourage feelings of productivity.

Gardening

Rewarding pleasure can come from simple things—a single flower in a vase, a windowsill of African violets, or an outdoor bed of zinnias. Gardening, as a hobby, can give patients an intimate look at the beauty of nature.

Plants are personal things, they are dependent upon the grower. Caring for something, such as a plant, watching it change and grow can stimulate feelings of usefulness and accomplishment, and strengthen the self-esteem of the patient.

Plants can grow indoors or outdoors, depending upon the patients' interests, capabilities, available space and the weather. Ambulatory patients may be able to give daily care to outdoor gardens, while wheelchair or bedridden patients can care for indoor plants.

A good indoor project is planting a bottle garden. Gallon wine bottles or salad oil bottles with wide necks can be used. Plants that can withstand moist soil and high humidity, such as small-leafed ivies, ferns, or moss are adaptable plants. They can be carefully eased through the neck of the bottle into a basic potting soil mix. Bottle gardens require little care, are inexpensive projects, and offer a therapeutic reward to patients.

Movies

Movies can provide a passive, relaxing form of entertainment that appeals to a variety of patients. The physically handicapped can also benefit from movies. Focusing on sounds and music, the blind or visually impaired can enjoy movies. Hard-of-hearing or deaf patients may like silent films such as the Charlie Chaplin Classics. Selection of films should be based upon the background, interests, and age of the patients. Films with simple plots, familiar settings, and lively music are popular favorites.

Movies can be an inexpensive media. Excellent films can be borrowed free of charge from local public libraries or other community sources. Volunteers or staff may be amateur photographers and gladly show their films or slides at the nursing home. An example of such an activity was when the Home Director of Nurses showed her vacation slides of Hawaii. The patients were eager to learn and share her travel experiences. Following the slide presentation, the patients informally discussed such concepts as food, customs, and climate. The activity proved to be an enlightening exchange of ideas.

Games

Games can add fun and gaiety to the lives of the nursing home patients. They are effective techniques for provoking mental activity, encouraging socialization, and promoting physical exercises. The following are several examples of different types of game activities which can be utilized by alert, confused, or handicapped patients.

Beachball Game

Senile, mentally confused, or nonambulatory patients can sit in a circle and pass a large colorful beachball to one another. Some patients do not know or remember names of others who share their same home. As they throw the ball, they can call out the person's name who will be catching the ball and thus become familiar with their names and enhance socialization skills.

Bean Bag Toss

Bean bags made in craft workshops can be thrown into a brightly decorated basket or box. Bedridden men with the use of only one arm can participate in such an activity. Rules can be modified to meet the needs of the individual.

Table Games

Some games can offer a mental challenge for alert patients. Such games as cards, dominoes, checkers, and chess involve skill and competition. Occasional tournaments can add excitement to the program. Special cards and games can be purchased from the American Foundation for the Blind to include the visually handicapped in familiar table games. Enlarged cards, Braille dominoes, and bingo sets are available.

Bingo

Bingo is one of the most popular indoor games among the aged. It involves no skill and little concentration. For this reason confused patients can be included. Bingo can be played inside patients' rooms if they are unable to come to the activity area. Organizations, community groups, or private businesses may donate small gifts such as pens, rain bonnets, combs, or stationery that can be used as prizes. Winning a small prize can be an enjoyable experience. Patients with hearing problems or visual handicaps can be seated next to partners who can help them play their cards. Refreshments can be served and a simple bingo game can turn out to be a spontaneous reason for a party.

Outdoor games

Ambulatory patients can walk outdoors and participate in such games as rubber horseshoes, quoits, shuffleboard, or croquet. These games encourage socialization and promote physical exercise, which is still essential for older people.

Music

Music can play a large part in the recreation program. Listening to music, making it, and sharing talents with others are creative activities that bring much happiness to the elderly. Music has much social value since it brings people together. Beginning, successful music activities can include the following:

Sing-Alongs

Get a large group of patients together and sing a variety of songs. Familiar songs, such as "Irish Eyes," "Let Me Call You

Sweetheart," or "He's Got the Whole World in His Hands," may bring back many pleasant memories to the aged. Although the old familiar songs are popular, the aged may also enjoy modern folk songs and selections from musicals. Song sheets printed in large type can be used to introduce new songs. Group singing can strengthen group morale and encourage feelings of togetherness.

Music Appreciation Groups

Public libraries are excellent sources for borrowing records of all kinds. Groups can gather in the activity room, or a phonograph can be taken into patients' rooms to include the roombound. Playing selected records may have more meaning if information is provided beforehand about the composer and how the piece was written. After records have been played, discussion of the music can begin.

Talent Shows

Utilize the elderly in planning and presenting a talent show. Many patients may sing well, play musical instruments, recite poetry, or tell jokes. One man of 94 years was very confused, but he could vividly recall lines from Shakespeare. He proved to be an enjoyable asset to our talent show.

Music may mean more to the visually handicapped than to patients who can see. Music can be educational as well as recreational for the visually impaired. Talking Books, which are long-playing records, can be an effective means of stimulating educational growth for the blind. They can be obtained from sources such as the Commission on Aid to the Blind.

Outings

Nearly everyone likes to visit places, to see things, and to enjoy new experiences. Outings can acquaint patients with what the changing world is like today. Living in a nursing home can promote feelings of social isolation or alienation from the world "outside." A sense of being "out of touch" with society can be witnessed by some patients. By getting out of the home and being exposed to various living situations, the aged can strengthen their ties with society.

Outings can include numerous types of activities. A walk to the barber shop to get a haircut, a bus ride to a nearby park, or a visit to a church supper are examples of interests that provide cultural exposure as well as simple entertainment. Reduced ticket rates and transportation fares enable the feasibility of such trips at an inexpensive cost.

The therapeutic benefits of outings can be illustrated by a personal experience. One warm spring day, I took a small group of men to a baseball game. The ballpark was sponsoring a special Senior Citizens Day, and tickets were available at a low half-price rate. A quiet, shy man about seventy years old "came out of his shell" while at the game. Excited to be at the game, he began to relate his past experiences. I learned that he had been a bat boy for the Boston Braves many years ago. During the game he began to discuss the ballplayers and coaches that he had personally known; he also compared what baseball was like then and how he felt it had changed.

For him the outing had brought back many fond remembrances. Weeks later he kept talking about his pleasurable experiences while on our trip. I followed up his interest in baseball by borrowing books on the subject from the public library. This outing had regenerated his confidence and interest to participate in other recreation activities.

Community Involvement

A final step in implementing purposeful program planning is opening the nursing home doors to the community. The pragmatic values of a community volunteer program include providing services which the nursing home could not otherwise afford.

A volunteer service program can add meaning to the lives of the aged. Volunteers can give their friendships, understanding, talents, time, and energy and provide rewarding experiences for the aged to cherish. Some patients may have no outside visitors to brighten their days; a volunteer can fill this void in an elderly person's life. Community volunteers can give services and programs, thus activity costs are kept minimal. Examples are:

Entertainment

Musical entertainment for holiday or birthday parties can be supplied by choruses and instrumental groups from schools, senior citizen clubs, or church groups. The aged welcome a wide range of types of entertainment. Folk guitarists, senior citizen square dance groups, and minstrel shows are popular favorites.

Fulfilling the Spiritual Need

Religion is an integral part of the patients' lives. Faced with advancing age and declining health, older persons rely on religion to bring hope and faith for their tomorrow. Before coming to a nursing home, many patients had religious affiliations, and these should not be severed.

Religion can be a means of strengthening involvement with the community. If medically possible, patients can be encouraged to attend local churches, where they can make new friends and become active in church functions such as bazaars and church socials. Scheduled visits by the clergy can be set up in the nursing home. An example of an effective religious program was when a volunteer minister held weekly Bible-study classes. In an informal discussion group, patients exchanged ideas about the books and themes of the Bible, they questioned the meanings of prayers and sang favorite hymns. The activity proved to be worthwhile and attempted to fulfill their spiritual needs. Church groups may enjoy becoming active in nursing homes. One example was when a local group came to the home, picked up patients, and escorted them to an Easter service and later provided a church supper. The patients were so excited that community residents, who cared, were anxious to make their day a little happier.

Enjoying the life ahead for those who live in nursing homes can be attained by recreation therapy. Low budget programs, as previously described, can fulfill the needs of older people. The success of a recreation program is not entirely dependent on the amount of available funding. Creative leadership and utilization of resources can, to a great extent, offset shoestring budgets and provide many therapeutic rewards for elderly persons.

BIBLIOGRAPHY

McGlaun, Mable D.: *A Handbook for Recreation in the Modern Nursing Home.* Garland, B-Mac Publications, 1972.

Merrill, Toni: *Activities for the Aged and Infirm.* Springfield, Thomas, 1967.

Thompson, Morton: *Starting a Recreation Program in Institutions for the Ill or Handicapped Aged.* New York, National Recreation Association, 1960.

Townsend, Claire: *Old Age: The Last Segregation,* New York, Bantam Books, 1971.

SECTION V
APPROACHES IN THERAPEUTIC RECREATION

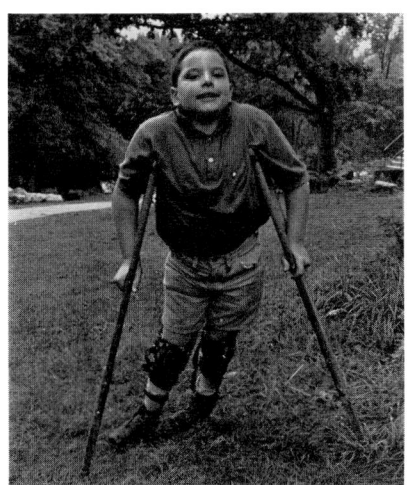

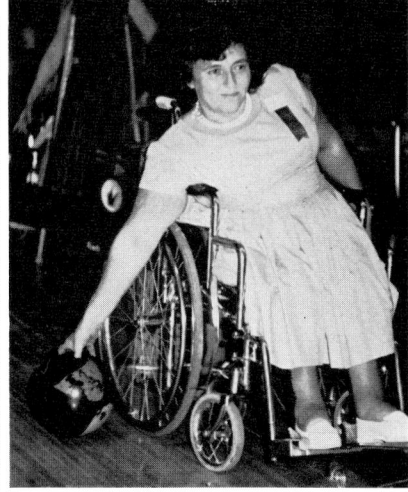

Top photo courtesy of
Cliff House Nursing Home,
Winthrop, Massachusetts.
Bottom photo courtesy of
Easter Seal Society for Crippled
Children and Adults of
Massachusetts, Inc.

Top photo courtesy of
Charles V. Hogan Regional Center.
Bottom photo courtesy of the
Indoor Sports Club, Inc.,
an International Club for the
Physically Disabled.

CHAPTER 10

INVESTIGATING MUSIC IN A THERAPEUTIC CAPACITY

CHRISTINE A. MEDA

THERAPY, THE NOUN, is defined as the art and science of treatment or rehabilitation which uses a structured format or orientation, supported by a body of knowledge, conducted by a trained person and administered with an awareness of goals and needs of the patient.[1] Using music as a therapeutic means has been experimented with and has shown positive results ... enough to warrant the establishment of the National Association for Music Therapy.

Music therapy can be broken down into three general categories of use: physical, expressive and/or emotional, and diversional.

Physical

People often connect the emotional and diversional aspects, but rarely consider the physical portion. Much experimenting has been done with the cerebral palsied child, who, experiencing lack of motor control, has found increased control through the physical use of music. An occupational therapist by the name of Barbara Denenholz has done research in this area. Some of her findings are incorporated into the following chart:[2]

Instrument	Body Part
Keyboard instrument	Movement of shoulder blades toward each other which activates the abductor and elevator muscles

---

1. Gerald Cohen and O. L. Gericke, Music therapy assessment, *Journal of Music Therapy*, IX:164, 1972.

2. Juliette Alvin, *Music for the Handicapped Child*. London, Oxford University Press, 1965, pp. 78-81.

Vertical chimes	Develops hand coordination including grasping, reaching, releasing
Guitar, autoharp, and woodwind instruments	Muscles of fingers which move joints nearest the wrist
Singing	Relaxes facial, palatal and laryngeal muscles
Woodwind instruments	Respiratory muscles Improves breathing Dental formation Defective mouth

In addition, S. Licht has found:[3]

Instrument	*Action*	*Part*
Piano	All	Fingers
Ukelele	Extension	Fingers
Piano	All but adduction	Thumb
Piano	Flexion-extension	Wrist
Guitar	Pronation-supination	Elbow
Violin	Flexion-extension	Elbow
Xylophone	All motions	Neck
Bass viol	All motions	Back
Organ	Abduction-adduction	Hips
Pianola	Flexion-extension	Knees
Parlor organ	Flexion-extension	Ankles

John D. McKee, born with spastic limbs, describes his situation as a young boy:

> My drumming resulted from not being able to play the clarinet. . . . For a long time my left hand did all the work . . . with practice, however, my right hand became more useful and drumming gave that spastic hand more strength and direction than it had ever before . . . my right hand is responsive enough so that I could get a satisfactory roll out of a drum.[4]

---

3. Robert Lundin, *An Objective Psychology of Music*, 2nd ed. New York, Ronald, 1967, p. 317.

4. Alvin, *op. cit.*

A "Music Therapy Project for Psychotic Children Under the Age of Seven" was developed at the University of Pennsylvania. One six-year-old child, by the name of Rosita, was tested. She was a dreamer, had minimal speech, involuntary repetition of speech and would continue to knot shoelaces or pieces of string.[5]

Therapy started with Rosita beating a drum to the therapist's piano playing. She didn't understand, at first, but as the two weekly sessions (10 minute duration) continued she made progress. She reached a point of imitation and then stopped on that level (familiar occurrence with autistic children). After five months, she started working again and reached the point of playing musical games with alertness. Finally she worked up to a point of excitement that caused her to break into song. This evolved into communicating freely, improving vocabulary, changing behavior and increasing alertness with her family.

"In all exercise the importance is on making a person think,"[6] which is what happens in musical activity. A handicapped person must eventually become aware of the beat and how to remain with it, therefore, forgetting about his disability. Simultaneously, the enjoyment of using the instrument or singing causes a more relaxed feeling and removes the fear which creates tension and nervousness in the patient.

Expressive and/or Emotional

In this area music made much headway since music itself is a form of expression based on emotion. The following specific examples have been tested with positive results:[7]

Anger

>Wagner: "Song to the Evening Star" from *Tannhauser*
>Brahms: "Lullaby"
>Nevin: "The Rosary"
>Debussy: "Clair de Lune"

---

5. Paul Nordoff and Clive Robbins, *Music Therapy for Handicapped Children.* New York, Rudolf Steiner Publications, 1965, pp. 86-88.

6. Alvin, *op. cit.,* p. 120.

7. Lundin, *op. cit.*

Depression
- Beethoven: *Egmont* Overture
- Bizet: Suite from *Carmen*
- Debussy: "Iberia"
- Haydn: *The Creation*

Fatigue
- Bach: Coffee Cantata
- Britten: "Peter Grimes"
- de Falla: "Nights in the Gardens of Spain"
- Handel: *Water Music*

Jealousy
- Bach: Cantata No. 21
- Bellini: Overture to *Norma*
- Copland: "Rodeo"
- Debussy: *La Mer*

Anxiety States
- Chopin: Preludes
- Strauss: Waltzes
- Schubert: Songs (Cheerful)
- Verdi: Melodic arias from operas

A three-and-a-half-year-old boy by the name of Russell, was tested with music at the University of Pennsylvania.[8] He had no speech and if a change in environment occurred he would fly into a tantrum. His one repeated action was rhythmically rocking in a chair, half humming, half grunting. His sessions started with a group of three children. The therapist started playing the piano and Russell chose a chair furthest from the piano, but he rocked away again. The therapist tried to play a tempo which corresponded to his movements. Intrigued, Russell rocked back to the piano and remained there for the rest of the session.

Along with playing the piano, the therapist sang in a chant style. Over a period of time, Russell's grunting became sustained tones and even started to change pitch in response to the thera-

---
8. Nordoff, *op. cit.,* pp. 90-94.

pist. This led to harmonization within the key feeling. At this point, the therapist felt he had established enough rapport with Russell to help him step to a new level of activity. He offered him a small drum and zylophone, but Russell would not take the mallet and expressed his rage in song—not using words, but melodic-rhythmic phrases. Russell then started beating the drum, cymbal and zylophone with enthusiasm and his future looked promising.

Diversional

The third division of music therapy is the diversional aspect —providing entertainment with or without actual participation. The musical taste of patients must be determined and then various groups asked to perform, i.e. jazz, country western, rock 'n' roll, hard rock, etc. This involves no participation from the patient unless the musical group incorporates them in their concert.

The sing-along is a diversional activity which does include participation. The patients can join in group singing, playing instruments and/or performing individually or in groups of two or three. The feeling of pleasure and joy are reinforced through participating and visualizing the expressions and emotions of others in the group.

Music therapy can be used at any age level. In the past two months, I have been working with geriatric patients and slowly developing a program using music as therapy. This has been initiated both on the individual level and the group level.

With geriatric patients, the major problem is inhibition and withdrawal from people and activity. Since music is an expression this problem must be overcome before anything else is accomplished.

The initial contact with a patient is the most crucial because an opinion of you can be formulated which is difficult to change. This opinion often determines whether the elderly will trust you enough to want to join in either individual or group activities. Once trust is established, I decide on the activity that would help in rehabilitation based on diagnosis (read before meeting the patient), expressed interest of patient and background.

For instance, I have a 65-year-old patient, Walter, whose diagnosis includes Paget's disease and muscular dystrophy. After talking with him, I found out he played jazz piano forty years ago. I asked him if he would like to try playing the piano again and he agreed to it. Considering how well he played forty years ago, how much he would remember, his physical ability and his musical taste, I chose an easy version of the "Merry Widow Waltz." It was a favorite of his generation and had a definite ¾ feeling.

At our first meeting, I realized Walter didn't remember much and that he had done most of his playing by ear. I established a number system for the notes that corresponded with the keyboard. This also was easier to read as Walter has glaucoma. We had to develop a position for him to sit at the piano in his wheelchair. Fortunately, this was easily remedied by removing the bottom board of the piano.

Walter had complete use of his left hand, but only the dexterity of one finger and thumb of his right. In the first few sessions he favored his left hand completely, but as he became more confident and relaxed his right hand came more into play. We are now working on keeping a steady beat through the entire song and have added three new songs (simplified versions) to his repertoire: "On Top of Old Smokey," "I Dream of Jeanie with the Light Brown Hair" and "Autumn Leaves." The exercise which he receives helps to maintain his physical level and keep his interest level high.

Another patient, Tom, had to be approached differently. He is seventy years old and has a fractured hip. I met with him several times and he was very withdrawn and unresponsive. Finally, at the third session he told me that he played violin for six years and that his favorite conductor was Mantovani. I obtained a record player and some Mantovani records to keep in his room. His initial reaction was one of appreciation, but also embarrassment because I was fussing over him. As an end result, he rekindled an interest in music and gained trust in me. He has been joining in group activities ever since.

Once a rapport is established with a patient on an individual basis, I try to get them interested in our group activities, some of which follow:

Physical activity through music
> "Pass-the-present" which is similar to musical chairs. The object is to unwrap the present to music with each person undoing it a little. The person with the present when the music stops is out and the person who unwraps the last portion of the present gets to keep it. In their excitement to unwrap the gift, they forget their handicaps.
>
> Rhythm band—playing percussion instruments to music of various tempos and getting the patients to beat in time and eventually improvise with the music.
>
> A square dance having the volunteers push the patients in wheel-chairs.

Expressive activity through music
> Musicals—having patients take the part of one character in the script and play the songs as they occur in the script—depending on the patient, they may want to sing the songs too. This could be performed for other patients.

Diversional activity through music
> Sing-alongs—using songs of their generation and supplying the words, accompaniment and percussion instruments for their use.
>
> Concerts—having outside groups come in and perform for the patients. Make sure the group plays music of interest to the audience and to which they can relate.
>
> Opera synopsis—reading the synopsis of various operas and playing the more well-known arias from them.
>
> Staff show—having the staff put on a show is very enjoyable as the patients certainly can relate to the group of performers.

Through trained personnel, organized procedures, and stated goals geared to the needs of the patients, music can be used as a therapy. The examples which I have cited show how it can be used in all three areas: physical, expressive and/or emotional, and diversional not only on the pediatric level, but also on the geriatric level. With positive results being constantly documented from experimentation, music will continue to grow and prove itself in a therapeutic capacity.

BIBLIOGRAPHY

Alvin, Juliette: *Music for the Handicapped Child*. London, Oxford University Press, 1965.

Cohen, Gerald and Gericke, O. L.: Music therapy assessment. *J Music Ther*, IX:164, 1972.

Lundin, Robert W.: *An Objective Psychology of Music*, 2nd ed. New York, Ronald Press, 1967.

Nordoff, Paul and Robbins, Clive: *Music Therapy for Handicapped Children*. New York, Rudolf Steiner Publications, 1965.

CHAPTER 11

WHAT CAN I BE? MUST I BE ME?

JACALYN HAMADA

ANY PHYSICAL OR MENTAL disability from the slightest limitation to the most confining illness is restrictive on both the individual and his development, however, in all situations one can experience the world around through dramatic play and games. This aspect of recreational therapy is unfortunately too often overlooked. For instance, Charley, the recreation therapist, thinks of recreation only in terms of sports, artistic endeavors such as crafts, group activities such as cards and games, passive participation such as listening to music or watching television. Oh, Charley! What happened to dramatics? Dramatics can be any one or all these things. Charley thinks that "that drama stuff takes too much planning, rehearsals, and work . . . can't be bothered with it." The world of dramatic play rarely reaches the stage; it does, however, use some of the training techniques of acting to achieve its goals.

Drama is all around, it's here, it's there, it's everywhere. Regardless of age, educational background, sex, IQ, or physical ability, dramatic games and fun can be used in every recreation program.

With very young children, or older children with slow learning abilities, creative dramatics can be a new world to explore. What exactly is creative dramatics? "Oh, that's when someone reads a story and kids act it out." Wrong again, Charley. Acting out stories can be used in creative session but, in fact, creative dramatics explores one's senses and responses to stimuli. These responses are then perhaps channeled through the imagination and may take many different forms.

Perhaps a look at some dramatic games and fun for children of all ages (four to 104 years of age) could best illustrate the flexibility of this addition to the recreation program. Remember, there are very few rules; however, one rule should never be forgotten: there is no wrong response because there are no set expectations.

Relaxation Games

This game is very useful at the beginning of a dramatic session; it can also come in handy in the middle of a session that may have lost its focus. Relaxation is an individual process that can be directed by a group leader. Participants should lie on the floor with hands at their sides and relax. The leader may vary this technique with the group. Some of the most effective methods are the closing of eyes, tensing and relaxing different areas of the body, listening to the sounds around, or turning on one's stomach and listening to the heart beat.

The leader might choose to stop after relaxation and completely change the environment or he might use part of the relaxation exercises as a transition to subsequent parts of the program. For instance, after listening to the sounds around, the leader may direct the group to picture whatever made the noise (an airplane, a passing truck or crickets): then he could ask the participants to either become that object or ride or fly that object to a certain place which he describes.

These sessions may be a series of independent games and exercises or they may have a theme or a thread that will continue throughout one entire session or a series of sessions.

Circle Games

Circle games are fun because every participant shares equally in the activity. Almost any activity can be transformed into a circle shape. The learning of names is most enjoyable in a circle. The leader may have a special sign that calls the group into a circle without verbal direction, e.g. an extended hand or three claps. The participants gather in a circle and the leader explains the guidelines: each participant will introduce himself first and then repeat the names of those who have preceded him. If someone forgets a name the entire circle is begun again. This is most appropriate because those at the beginning have fewer names to remember while those at the end have the benefit of hearing the names over and over. Listen as the leader begins: "I'm Sally"; person to her left, "I'm Kent, she's Sally, I'm Kent"; person to his left, "I'm Nick, she's Sally, he's Kent, I'm Nick." An added stipulation can be a rhythm to the chanting of the names. Two slaps to the knees (I'm Sally) and two claps (a pause) works well.

Another circle game can be the passing of objects or animals. The leader will choose an animal and hold it, pet it, or relate to it in some fashion. He then will pass it to the next person; however, as the animal is passed it is transformed into whatever the recipient deems it to be. All circle games can go on forever or the leader may choose to end the activity after one round.

Other popular circle games are pass-around stories. Each participant may add a single word, a phrase or a sentence. The structure should be indicated by the leader. The story may then be retold by one participant, acted out by each participant, or acted out by the group.

Stimuli Response

Media is quite an effective stimulant. Music, color, lights, art or pictures all may open up endless hours of fun. Reactions may be channeled through a mood response, a literal interpretation of the stimulus or a combination of both. If the leader has a tape of woodsy sound effects, the participants could become whatever is making the effects (wind, rain, trees, crickets) or be someone experiencing these things (feeling the wind and rain, hiding behind the trees, chasing the crickets). Perhaps the participants will react to a modern painting; the reaction is one of sadness. The participant may then either tell or act out whatever he feels caused the sadness.

Creative games serve not only as entertainment in this aspect but also as a part of growth and personality development. Participants can explore different roles without endangering their conception of themselves or the expectations set upon them by others. Whenever it is possible, as here in the stimuli response, the leader should encourage the participants to try as many roles or behaviors as the individual wishes. Never, never force a role that may be threatening; the participant will set his own limits. The leader may expand these limits or remove them but it is up to the individual to pursue the new avenues.

Transformations

The leader, gifted with a very special magical power, is able to transform any or all of the participants of the group into the same or different beings or objects. A magic wand, word or movement may be needed to make the transformation official. ZAP!! Everyone is a dog. ZAP!! Half are now cats. The group is free to interact with one another or respond individually. This is very successful with pre-teenagers. Older participants working in a small group or as individuals may transform themselves into an immobile object or a working machine. Each group or individual may then share the object.

Games such as transformations are not limited to simple sterile games but can be combined with stimulus response activities. For example, there is a song called "I'm Being Eaten by a Boa Constrictor" (Peter, Paul and Mary). The words are simple and the tune is easily picked up.

> Oh I'm being eaten by a boa constrictor, a boa constrictor, a boa constrictor.
> Oh I'm being eaten by a boa constrictor and I don't like it very much!
> Oh no! Oh no! He's at my toe. He's at my toe.
> Oh gee! Oh gee! He's at my knee. He's at my knee.
> Oh fiddle! Oh fiddle! He's at my middle. He's at my middle.
> Aw, heck! Aw, heck! He's at my neck. He's at my neck!
> Oh dread! Oh dread! He's at my (muffled noise).

The participants may sing the song several times. Then each individual may be eaten by the boa constrictor; after that the participant may be the boa constrictor. The group could then be the boa constrictor collectively and eat the leader.

As with all dramatic games the opportunities are limitless. If the leader will open his mind and let his imagination be free, the group will profit and the session will be successful.

Nonverbal communication

Isolating different parts of the body, the group may experiment with the expression of thoughts or actions without words.

There are common signs used daily (a finger to the lips, the OK sign, the upheld hand for stop) and the limitless subtle movements which the group may take an entire session to explore. Using a towel or a portable blackboard, the leader should direct the participants to communicate, individually or in groups, a story with their bare feet. The feet can be objects or human feet expressing the attitude or action of the wearer. The skit or expression should be shared with the group. This same activity works equally well with hands appearing on top of a desk or only facial expressions. A variation on this theme is to have the group close their eyes and have individuals or groups tell a story with sounds only. This is similar to mime.

Not So Verbal Communications

Using one's voice but employing nonsense or gibberish to tell a story or participate in a conversation can be fun. The leader may direct the group to use only babytalk or perhaps the ABC's. This exercise emphasizes expression over verbal content.

Creative dramatic sessions such as these can be a series of exercises and game- or theme-oriented. For example, the circus is always fun. The music of the calliope may provide the stimulation for one part of the session; a story or a book of pictures may be the source for the next activity. The participants may all become a carousel after being circus-goers riding on a carousel. Groups may become different parts of the circus (high-wire acts or sideshow exhibits). Other successful themes are The Zoo, Mythology, The Senses, and Colors.

In planning a session, one does not have to stick strictly with the theme. It is most advantageous to plan well for a session. Participants often lose interest if they have to wait while a leader sets up or looks at his notes. The structure of a session should be well planned, however, it must be flexible. The leader must be flexible. Sometimes an exercise just won't work. Don't ram it down the participants' throats! Have a few reserve ideas to call on. Those old faithful stand-bys always are great in a pinch. If the group does not feel settled or is too noisy, the leader may either try relaxation or following through on the impulse of the group. If the participants are restless, run them around the room a few times (with guidance) or if they are noisy, have them make very loud noises and very soft noises. Then after recapturing their interest, proceed with the plans. Activities almost always take longer than anticipated. If the clock is running short, eliminate games rather than hurry the participants through a session because it was planned to have eight activities and only four have been done. It is very unsatisfying not to be able to complete an activity. On the other hand if something is working well, don't beat it into the ground. Just after an exercise has peaked, begin a new variation or new activity. Keep the interest level high.

Sessions need not always be planned; spontaneity can be just as successful. On a hike through the woods, returning from a museum trip or just rainy-day boredom, each of these could trigger a most enjoyable session. Reenacting what one has seen, reacting to what one hears, or just simply following the whim of imagination can be very exciting. Don't be afraid to try these exercises and games. They are very safe for the participants because they require neither a correct answer nor an innate talent.

More formal dramatic efforts won't hurt a recreation therapy program. Skits, plays, radio shows and play readings are but a few of the many areas which can be tried. However, there are many fine books on these areas. And don't forget puppetry!

When dealing with special populations, a recreation therapist need only use his head in adapting any of these exercises. For example, with the wheelchair patient one would not use a foot isolation exercise for nonverbal communication; a hand isolation or puppetry game would be appropriate. A child with a speech impediment may shy away from the group if everything is in "normal" speech; for this child some nonsense conversation, animal sounds, and object transformations may give him confidence in himself and encourage him to become a member of the group.

After overcoming his initial fear of creative dramatics and dramatic games, Charley found them a most complementary addition to his recreation therapy program. A recreation therapist need never be faced with the question, "What can I be? Must I be me?"

CHAPTER 12

VOLUNTEER WORKREATION: A UNIQUE THERAPEUTIC MODEL

Gwen Gutter

WHEN AN INDIVIDUAL working for the benefit of society abdicates all monetary concerns, that individual becomes known as a volunteer. For the volunteer, work should be a self-satisfying experience since it is leisure time that is being donated; and leisure, being synonymous with recreation, should always be pleasurably stimulating.

The motives which propel an individual into volunteer work are numerous. Some motives are more humanistic than others, but generally, all produce self-gratification in some way. In a study on job motivation, it was found that the "profoundest motivation to work comes from the recognition of individual achievement and from the sense of personal growth in responsibility."[1] These two drives are just as applicable to the volunteer as to the paid worker in the above-mentioned study. The achievement of these motives makes work a satisfying experience, thereby making the experience recreative for the volunteer.

Volunteer work as a form of recreation has much therapeutic value for both the contributing person and for the receiving party. In the following study, one organization's approach to the volunteer system was observed and will be reviewed for its total effectiveness.

The volunteer workreation study was conducted on a local chapter of a worldwide organization known as "The Process." The Process, founded in London, England in the mid-1960's by Robert de Grimston, is a religious order that has expanded to the United States and Canada where it claims headquarters in five

---

1. Frederick Herzberg, Bernard Mausner, and Barbara Bloch Snyderman, *The Motivation to Work.* New York, Wiley, 1959, p. 125.

major cities. The organization is financially dependent on money raised through sales of Process literature and on donations. The philosophical vehicle that determines Processean activities stems from the teachings of Christ's golden rule, "Do unto others as you would have others do unto you." The Processean interpretation of this rule, "The Universal Law," follows that "As you give, so shall you receive."[2]

Processeans and their followers are individuals from various backgrounds, many who have come to The Process desperate for change in their lives. These people, "an incredible mixture of the intellectually curious with the desperate,"[3] dedicate their lives to aiding mankind through their volunteer services. Via the Processean route, these individuals help themselves while helping others, thereby making work a self-gratifying experience which is dually therapeutic.

The Process chapter house is maintained by the communal efforts of its members and followers. Home front activities include work in such areas as housekeeping, secretarial duties, carpentry, operating a free kitchen and clothing shop open to the public, and even babysitting for the children of the Processean families. Although many of the work projects within the house involve laborious time, these dedicated workers describe their tasks as recreational and fulfilling. Many of these individuals take on tasks in which they can best channel their productivity, thereby manifesting personal achievement and a feeling of contribution. Their greatest rewards come to them in the form of a mental and spiritual growth, for by contributing to the maintenance of the organization these individuals provoke beneficial changes both within the organization and within themselves.

Another phase of Processean sustenance is their Street Ministry. This aspect of the organization serves numerous functions. It is composed of Process members who spend their days on busy public streets soliciting donations by selling Processean pamphlets

---

2. Robert de Grimston, *Donating*. Process Church of the Final Judgment, Toronto, p. 5.

3. John Lipsky, The Process: Carrying a torch for Lucifer. *The Real Paper*, November 29, 1972, p. 8.

and magazines. In their street contacts, as in all their contacts, Processeans are continuously reaching out to people. Through their short street encounters they aim to bestow upon other people the gifts that have been given to them, "which are gifts of knowledge and awareness and the growing freedom from conflict which those qualities bring."[4] One should not be misled into believing that the approach of the Processean is religious. Their approach is determined by the specific need of each particular person they encounter; and it is that need that the Processean attempts to deal with and hopefully satisfy. The general feeling of the members of the Street Ministry is that their main function often has little or nothing to do with the sale of a book. If their understanding can help a person more than a Processean pamphlet can, then they have accomplished their work.

Processeans are most active in yet another phase of public relations.

> On the basis that not everybody can come to a Process Chapter, Processeans take "Chapters" to the people, in the form of P-Cars. P-Cars are either large mobile units that can accommodate eight to twelve Processeans, or (since these are at the moment financially hard to come by) regular Chapter cars, which visit cities, towns and out-of-the-way places on regular circuits. In each town visited, a normal day can include visits to local authorities, civic and social bodies, and religious representatives; spreading the word to the townspeople; selling Church publications; speaking at schools and universities and local help organizations; presenting Process activities, and generally telling people about The Process and answering their questions.[5]

It should now be apparent that through their efforts to maintain and expand their organization, Processeans and their followers are continuously giving and receiving, a reciprocal act which is emotionally and spiritually therapeutic for them and for many of those with whom they make contact.

In the area of community social service, The Process conducts manifold volunteer projects which they refer to as "Mercy Mis-

---

[4]. Robert de Grimston, *Foundation*. Process Church of the Final Judgment, Toronto, p. 8.

[5]. Robert de Grimston, *Fax 'N Figgers*. Process Church of the Final Judgment, Toronto, p. 5.

sions." Within the past year Processean volunteer programs have expanded to over one hundred major cities of the United States and Canada.[6] An enormous variety of programs are in progress, many which include daily visits to hospitals, mental institutions, orphanages, old age homes, prisons, drug and alcoholic rehabilitation centers, reform schools and other such institutions.

Programs for each institution depend on that population's particular needs and on the interests and capabilities of the volunteering Processean.[7] "My goal is to give contact and life to people," states Brother Ed, a Process volunteer who regularly visits an institution for the mentally ill. During his hourly visits there is no limit on the scope of what he can give. Whatever need manifests itself at the time is what is dealt with. On one visit Ed may be confronted with a mentally retarded male adult needing assistance in personal grooming; consequently, on that visit Ed helps the man to shave. Sometimes Ed arrives finding a high energy level present in a group of patients. His instincts tell him that these people are in need of a pleasure walk, and thus the activity is decided upon. Ed often assists in the workshops where many of the patients are taught simple work skills in an assembly line fashion. Whatever his daily contribution, Ed feels he is at the very least giving social contact to individuals who are rarely, if at all, visited by others for this purpose.

For some members of the institutionalized society, outside social contact is so vital that Processeans have developed a "Personal Volunteer System." Aimed at social rehabilitation, the personal volunteer works on a one-to-one basis with an individual who is unable to function socially among the other members of the institution. The goal of the volunteer is to help this individual gain acceptance of him/herself, which in turn should help his/her relationships with others. To accomplish this goal the volunteer must accept this person and truly become a friend to him/her. Such is the situation in which Sister Lisa became a personal

---

6. Catherine Ives, The quiet revolution. *The Processeans,* June:42, 1973.
7. *Ibid.,* p. 43.

volunteer to Sandy, a 33-year-old mentally retarded woman. Lisa's story follows:

> When I met Sandy first, she had very little confidence. It seemed she was always crying and weeping about something. She felt lost and very alone in the world. People used to refer to Sandy as one of the most difficult cases. What seemed like rejection at first was in fact a test of me, but trust was built up over a period of time. It's one of the most satisfying things I've ever done in my life.

It took Lisa over a year to reach Sandy, but her determination was strong. Now Sandy visits Lisa on weekends. Taking part in social functions outside the institution as well as within, Sandy now displays a confidence which a year ago would never have seemed possible.[8]

Bringing entertainment to the institutionalized is another Processean program that has been most successful. "The Rock of Ages" is a rock band that is comprised of approximately six to eight talented Processeans. These musicians aim at livening up the often monotonous days of many shut-ins. The band is eagerly welcomed by prisoners, hospitalized veterans, the mentally ill, the physically handicapped, and even by senior citizens! Occasionally visits are made to the institutions by a single guitarist who, with his familiar tunes, rarely fails to stir up a sing-along. Although appealing to most groups, this activity is especially enjoyed by prison inmates.

Other popular presentations made by talented Processeans are skits and plays. The Process writes and produces their productions, always keeping in mind the particular audience that will be viewing them.

Processean entertainment is by no means for the exclusive pleasure of people in institutions. "The Rock of Ages" makes regular performances on radio and television as well as in poorer neighborhoods and at rock concerts. They also provide entertainment for visitors of The Process chapter house.

There are several other Process projects that further express

---

8. The Process: It took about a year to get from Waltham, Massachusetts, to Cambridge. *The Processeans, 00*:47, 1973.

the humanistic qualities characteristic of the members of this organization. Free handouts of food and clothing are frequently made to needy individuals; at open air concerts, or just out in a local park, The Process often appears with a "Free Food" stand. Helping care for the animals at the local zoo is yet another (strange, but beautiful!) voluntary contribution made by The Process.

Not to be forgotten are the activities that take place within The Process chapter house itself. Open to all, at no charge, is The Process Coffee House. Here, free health food snacks accompanied by conversation, recreational games, and entertainment are always at hand. Counseling by Process members is also available to those who drop by with problems. Some of the special activities conducted within the chapter on a regular basis are telepathy circles, midnight meditations, and chant sessions.

The services of The Process within their own community and in other cities are obviously overwhelming. In terms of therapeutic value there are numerous positive effects for Processeans as well as for those they serve. Many Processean volunteers are highly educated people, trained in areas related to the volunteer work they perform. There are those however, whose educational backgrounds have been scant. Through the spiritual education they receive as members of The Process, this latter group finds purpose and satisfaction in volunteer work. Father Reuben, one of the Superiors of The Process describes the therapeutic pattern of some Processeans:

> There are many delinquent people who come to The Process needing acceptance. Some find friends here and decide they want to become part of The Process. This is only done by giving. By coming into contact with people who are more committed than they are, these new people begin to expand. Once into their work the changes are obvious. Each person has something of his own choice to contribute, and it is validated, accepted, and rewarded. Their greatest rewards are spiritual. They begin to feel like part of a family and community in which they are worthwhile contributing members. Their contacts in community-service help them to improve their relationships with all types of people. As a result, they become more confident of their acceptance by society.

As mentioned earlier, work for the volunteer should be satisfying and recreational. According to Father Lucius, a Master of The Process, "If it's not fun, there's something wrong." His concept of the ideal volunteer follows:

> The ideal volunteer is the person for whom the work doesn't seem like work. Because he doesn't do it for the wrong reasons, like he feels guilty and he has to make a sacrifice or do something virtuous. (Too many charitable institutions appeal—to my mind quite mistakenly—to people's guilt for their own well-being.) No, he does it for the right reasons, i.e. because he enjoys it, he gets pleasure out of it, it's fun, it's fulfilling, it's satisfying.[9]

In observations of and discussions with Process volunteers it became apparent that these dedicated individuals are all characteristic of the ideal volunteer described above by Father Lucius.

Considering the therapeutic value for those served by The Process, it should be obvious that the effects are monumental. With our institutions being overcrowded there is little opportunity for a patient to receive much personal attention. Through the efforts of The Process however, several are receiving care and concern from a society they have temporarily or permanently left, or for many, have never really been part of.

The Process organization is to be highly commended. It is unconcerned with the social recognition and prestige which unfortunately are the underlying motives of countless volunteers. The contributions made to society by The Process are of a humanistic quality which is the reason that its volunteer system is so admirable. When more volunteers take a lesson from The Process's Universal Law, "As you give, so shall you receive," work will then become both recreational and therapeutic to all concerned.

BIBLIOGRAPHY

de Grimston, Robert: *Donating*. Process Church of the Final Judgment, Toronto.

de Grimston, Robert: *Fax 'N Figgers*. Process Church of the Final Judgment, Toronto.

---

9. Ives, *op. cit.*, p. 43.

de Grimston, Robert: *Foundation*. Process Church of the Final Judgement, Toronto.

Herzberg, Frederick, Mausner, Bernard, and Snyderman, Barbara Bloch: *The Motivation to Work*. New York, Wiley, 1959.

Ives, Catherine: The quiet revolution. *The Processeans*, A Monthly Report. June, 1973, pp. 42-43.

Lipsky, Jon: The Process. Carry a torch for Lucifer. *The Real Paper*, Vol. 1, No. 18, November 29, 1972, pp. 1, 8-9.

The Process: It took about a year to get from Waltham, Massachusetts, to Cambridge. *The Processeans*, A Monthly Report. June, 1973, p. 47.

CHAPTER 13

DEVELOPING A VOLUNTEER PROGRAM IN THE THERAPEUTIC SETTING

Elise O'Brien

Q*uestion:* I am sincere, patient, cheerful, poised, tactful, sensitive, reliable, sympathetically understanding, and I love people. I played a very important role in the founding and development of America. I donate immeasurable amounts of time, energy and effort to the well-being of my fellow man. Who am I?

Answer: A volunteer worker.

Introduction

Before focusing on recreation volunteers in a therapeutic community, I believe a brief background of voluntary service would be of value. America's foundation was based on the spirit of help-the-other-fellow. Neighbors joined together to aid in the caring for the ill, to help in the harvesting of crops, or to help in the building of a barn or church. The opportunity to work with others during leisure time provided recreation and companionship for the settlers. As the communities developed and the population grew, joint efforts were needed to create services for specific groups of people who needed areas and facilities for recreational activities and meetings. This country's first recreational projects were started by a person or a small group who wanted to do something extra for the community's people, or sensed a need of additional activities in the church or in the neighborhood for educational, recreational, or social outlets. Professional workers first entered the scene when the programs, begun by volunteers, grew to the point where full-time workers or specialists were needed.[1]

---

1. *The Recreation Program.* Chicago, The Athletic Institute, 1963, p. 317.

Today volunteers and professionals work hand in hand striving to service more people. It is my intention in researching and writing this paper to discover how professional workers can help volunteers in a therapeutic setting become an integral part of a rehabilitation team. The professional worker has a responsibility to orient and prepare volunteers to achieve therapeutic goals through training, supervision, friendly discussion, and other methods. In considering the values of volunteer service, one must not only note the services rendered, but also the fact that volunteers frequently consider the donating of their service a major part of their own recreation.

The success or failure of a volunteer program depends on intelligent planning. Properly supervised and trained, regular volunteers become indispensable members of the recreation department staff. Because of their dependability, regularity and training, they enable the professional recreation staff to plan and operate a program of greater scope with more attention to individual patients than would be possible without the services of volunteers. The volunteer assignments should always be planned in detail, even before they are recruited; volunteers should be convinced they will be doing something useful—that a particular activity would not take place unless they were there.[2]

Volunteer Contributions

Volunteers make enumerable contributions to the therapeutic community. They relieve the professional staff of many minute details that do not require specialized training. They supplement and extend the program and services to new areas previously unexplored and make it possible to offer a wider variety of activities, more frequent sessions, and consequently a greater opportunity for free choice of activities among patients. Volunteers also provide a bridge between the patient and the community by helping to retain or renew contact with people and activities in the community. Volunteers, persons with unhurried or unpur-

---

2. Toni Merrill, *Activities for the Aged and Infirm.* Springfield, Thomas, 1967, p. 75.

chased time, contribute to patient morale in a unique way. Personal contact with a volunteer helps a patient realize there is someone who cares for him and is interested in him.

Types of Volunteers

There are many different types of volunteers participating in a well-run recreation department. Volunteer leaders are your experts in the fields of flower arranging, gardening, music, painting, reading, or sculpture who conduct programs for patients on a regularly scheduled basis. Volunteer aides are carefully selected and trained persons who wish to donate a few hours per week to work with patients, such as friendly visiting, writing letters or assisting in arts and crafts. Other volunteers serve not individually, but as groups, and they may sponsor social group activities or monthly social parties working with large groups of patients with bingo, birthday parties, picnics, special programs or outdoor events. Often volunteer groups will be invited to perform for the therapeutic community. Such performances may include dancing exhibitions, sing-alongs, plays, or magic shows. The professional worker should be at the door to greet the group on arrival, assist them with preparations, and stay with them throughout the duration of the program. As the volunteer group leaves, the professional worker thanks each member and if the program warrants it, arranges a date for a return visit. A Volunteer Entertainment Record card, such as the one to be found in the appendix, should be kept on file for reference.

Another type of volunteer is the college student who desires to help others, and at the same time gain valuable experience in preparation for professional work. Professional entertainers, sports personalities, and other celebrities become volunteers when they come to the hospital to visit and sometimes entertain the patients without charging a personal appearance fee. Other members of the hospital staff may also be interested in assisting with the recreation program during their leisure time. The opportunity to be associated with the healthy and happy aspects of their patients' lives in contrast to the pathological aspects with which they deal in their own professional capacities makes volunteering in recreation especially appealing.[3] Service volunteers are those persons who are occupied in clerical jobs, as library assistants or those who maintain or repair buildings and equipment. Some groups and individuals prefer to make their contribution to the recreation program in the form of materials and supplies rather than direct personal participation. Teenagers have great potential in volunteer service but they sometimes need painstaking training and supervision by the professional staff to assure progress toward the achievement of their potential.

Volunteers help to tear down the stigma of old age: preserving self-respect, sustaining tranquility, and cultivating friendships and interests outside the hospital are all a part of caring for the aged. Many community groups such as Senior Citizens, Golden Agers, or church groups meet regularly in rehabilitation centers, extended-care facilities and hospitals, extending invitations to patients to attend and participate in the groups.

Volunteer Recruitment and Screening

With leisure hours increasing the sources of volunteer power remain virtually untapped. The therapeutic community must take the initiative in recruiting volunteers from social and church organizations, service bureaus, and by word of mouth. The volunteer candidate is invited to the facility by the recreation therapist for an interview and to complete an application form. (See Appendix for an example of the form.) During the interview, the prospective volunteer is asked to describe his background, interests and abilities. A briefing on the patients, the philosophy of the recreation program, and finally a tour of the facility should be made. In addition to the traditional handbook, written guidelines for visitors and volunteers should be presented to the candidate for study. The actual decision on acceptance is made after the interview and is dependent upon the approval of both parties involved. In recruiting volunteers, retired people with extra time are often discovered with special talents and useful experience. These members of our older generation have

---

3. Virginia Frye and Martha Peters, *Therapeutic Recreation: Its Theory, Philosophy, and Practice.* Harrisburg, Stackpole Books, 1972, p. 169.

much else to offer: the sharing of their experiences and wisdom gained over the years and first-person tales of historical significance. It is important to remember that a volunteer is recruited to give a supplementary service, not to overcome staff shortages.

If a volunteer is to gain his recreation through service and if he is to serve a useful purpose, the professional has three obligations: selection; training; and supervision.[4] To insure effective volunteers, candidates must be screened very carefully. The professional worker needs to question a prospective volunteer's motives and evaluate the opportunities for the therapeutic community to fulfill them. Today many doctors, psychologists, social workers, and counselors are suggesting volunteer work for their clients as part of the prescribed treatment for various physical and emotional illnesses. This group of potential volunteers could represent a valuable work force if the professional staff member in charge plans the volunteers' orientation and training program skillfully. They can be effective, integral members of the therapeutic team if they are placed in the right jobs. Therefore, when assigning prospective workers it is essential to remember that the volunteer should fit the job; the job should not be tailored to fit the volunteer. Each specific job assignment should be in writing with a clear definition of job responsibilities and expectations for the information of all persons involved in the assignment.

Volunteer Orientation

The accepted volunteer will be asked to attend a general orientation at which time he should be introduced to the staff and instructed in his role in the program. Description of the facility, policies and an explanation of philosophy, admission procedures and the behavior and attitudes of the patients is necessary. In order to cover all of these points, it seems advisable to have different staff members—the Administrator, Director of Nurses, Medical Director, Social Worker and Therapeutic Recreation Specialist—give short meaningful talks to the volunteers. The reader is directed to Merrill's book *Activities for the Aged and Infirm,* for suggested outlines for these talks.

---
4. *The Recreation Program, op. cit.,* p. 321.

A necessary component of an effective volunteer program is keeping the staff informed about the volunteers, their contributions, and responsibilities within the facility. This orientation should be part of the professional staff's in-service training program.

Job design is the important responsibility of the recreation therapist, who must create jobs that are suitable for volunteers. Volunteer assignments must serve a real need of the hospital and, in the final analysis, provide better patient care. Assignments must not be busy work. Jobs designed for volunteers should vary as much as the volunteer group's own composition—for example: routine assignment vs. creative capacities.[5] If volunteers are to be useful to the program, dependability and punctuality should be emphasized. Should a volunteer be unable to work as scheduled, he would be expected to inform the recreation therapist of his absence as far in advance as possible, so that a substitute could be arranged.

Volunteer Training and Supervision

Koh suggests that the orientation to a job assignment be a three stage process:

1. Observation session: the volunteer notes responses of patients as well as techniques and procedures used by other members of the recreation team during an activity.
2. Supervised practice session (internship): during this time the recreation staff can assess the ability of the volunteer.
3. If a volunteer has shown promise of competence, he should be encouraged to work on his own with a minimum of supervision.[6]

Many hospitals have found it advisable to place prospective volunteers on probation for their first ten hours of hospital work. At the end of this period, he is either recommended for permanent assignment to the probationary job, transferred to another more suitable job, or withdrawn from volunteer work. If capable and skilled volunteers are to be retained, they must be

---

5. Mary Koh, Effective use of volunteers in a therapeutic recreation setting. *Ther Rec J, VI:*I:22, 1972.
6. *Ibid.,* p. 24.

challenged; if a volunteer feels he is needed for all he can give, he most often will give all he has.[7]

Workshops which attempt to teach volunteers simple skills helpful in making friendships, easy ways of bringing people together happily, reaching the lonely and depressed, the inactive and withdrawn, should be an important integral part of the training program.

Supervision is a continuous process which establishes self-confidence in a volunteer and helps to utilize his best capabilities. Volunteers should be enlisted to set up planned programs; aid in the transportation of patients to planned activities; assist patients when necessary in arts and crafts, games and other programs; serve as companions to those unable or unwilling to participate and attempt to stimulate their interests in various activities. Should a volunteer be unsure of a patient's ability to participate in an activity, he should contact the therapeutic recreation specialist immediately. All volunteers should also be clearly instructed that any medical or personal information learned about patients is confidential and that they should engage in only cursory comments about the patient with the staff and visitors.[8]

Recognition of Volunteers

Recognition, in the form of teas, luncheons, pins, news releases spotlighting volunteer services, photo displays showing them at work, and letters of appreciation are extremely important to volunteers. Special awards for hours contributed can develop into an annual event which serves three purposes: to honor the volunteer, to delight the patients, to publicize the hospital.

Termination of Volunteers

It is important to keep the standard of volunteer service at a high level. Therefore, the services of volunteers who ineffectively perform their duties should be terminated. It is the right of the volunteer to be told the reasons for his termination, some of

---
7. *Ibid.*
8. Dulcey B. Miller, *The Extended Care Facility: A Guide to Organization and Operation.* New York, McGraw-Hill, 1969, p. 269.

which might be poor health, behavioral inconsistency, poor work habits, unreliability, and/or an inability to accept supervision. The termination should conclude on a positive note: "It seems that the situation is difficult for you as well as for this hospital; it may be better if another volunteer assignment is arranged for you in another setting."[9] The professional worker in charge of volunteers has the responsibility to ascertain that the arrangement is finalized without hard feelings. Frequently volunteers terminate their affiliation with the facility for personal reasons, i.e. changing family demands, change of jobs or poor health. In all cases, a letter of appreciation from the hospital should be a part of the termination procedure regardless of the circumstances.

Conclusion

Indeed, when dealing with volunteers, human factors are the most important elements for the therapeutic recreation specialist to keep in the forefront of his mind. Respect, appreciation, communication, acceptance and patience are but a few of the intangibles that unite men in service to humanity. Hopefully volunteer workers will find, as they look back upon their lives, that some of their most rewarding moments have been spent in service to others.

APPENDIX

Volunteer Application Form[10]

.... Hospital

A. Personal Data
   1. Mr. Mrs. Miss ....
                        First   Initial   Last
   2. Street & No. ....
      City ....
   3. ....
             Office Phone   Home Phone
   4. Organizations ....

---

9. Koh, *op. cit.*, p. 38.
10. Merrill, *op. cit.*, pp. 76-78

5. Other special interests or training: ....
   ....
   ....
   ....
   ....
6. Car Available: ....
B. Desired Schedule of Services
   1. Contemplated duration of your offer of volunteer services:
      1 to 3 mos.... 3 to 6 mos.... 6 to 12 mos.... Indef....
   2. Time of day available:
      Morning.... Afternoon.... Evening.... All day....
   3. Days of Week Available:
      Sun...... Mon...... Tues...... Wed...... Thurs......
      Fri...... Sat......
   4. Schedule of Visits:
      Weekly..... Monthly..... Twice a Month.....
   5. If you are available only at times certain groups or individuals are scheduled, please insert the name of the group or individual ....
      ....
C. Areas of Service Based on Interest, Experience or Training
   Please Check
   1. Recreation:
      Take patients for walks.... write letters.... read....
      visit wards.... planning, directing and participating in party games.... crafts....
      Can you play checkers.... dominoes.... pinochle....
      rummy.... cards.... billiards.... flinch....
      Sponsor parties ....
      Can you direct group singing.... kitchen band.... play piano.... other instruments.........................
      Check hobbies or interests: patients' newspaper.... run a project.... nature study.... scrapbooks....
      Active games: bowling.... pool.... horseshoes.... others
      ....
   2. Hobbies
      Can you weave.... sew.... paint.... draw.... clay

model.... knit.... crochet.... woodwork.... leather work.... wood chip.... fly tying.... rug weaving.... thread a loom.... other arts or crafts ....

3. Beauty Parlor:
   Indicate Interest: give permanents.... wash.... hair settings.... manicure.... hair cuts....

4. Library
   Indicate Interest: reading aloud.... library magazine and book cart service.... lead discussion group.... library maintenance....

5. Clerical
   Indicate Interest: filing.... typing.... mimeographing....

6. Social Service
   Visit hospitalized patients on regular basis who do not have visitors.... Do you speak a foreign language?.... Which................

7. Chaplaincy
   Indicate Interest: conduct Bible reading classes.... sing hymns.... provide social atmosphere for religious holidays............
   Assist chaplain during services on wards and in the chapel............

8. Miscellaneous
   Indicate Interests: Receptionist.... escort service for patients.... mending at home or church.... conduct hospital tours.... furnish transportation for others.... furnish party treats or favors....

List desired activity in order of preference:

1. ....
2. ....
3. ....
4. ....

Additional information or suggestions:

1. ....
2. ....
3. ....
4. ....

State work or training which might be of value:
Date Filed: ....

Volunteer Entertainment Record Card[11]

Date:
Name of Group or Individual:
Contact Person:
Address:
Telephone:
Date and Time Expected:
Place:
Transportation:
Program:
Refreshments Provided by Group:
Refreshments Provided by Hospital:
Equipment Provided by Group:
Equipment Provided by Hospital:
Resident Attendance:
Evaluation by Worker:
Thank-You Letter Written by:
Date:
Date for Return Performance:

BIBLIOGRAPHY

The Recreation Program. Chicago, The Athletic Institute, 1963.
Frye, Virginia and Peters, Martha: *Therapeutic Recreation: Its Theory, Philosophy, and Practice.* Harrisburg, Stackpole Books, 1972.
Koh, Mary: Effective use of volunteers in a therapeutic recreation setting. *Ther Rec J,* Vol. VI, No. I, pp. 22-28, 1972.
Merrill, Toni: *Activities for the Aged and Infirm.* Springfield, Thomas, 1967.
Miller, Dulcy B.: *The Extended Care Facility: A Guide to Organization and Operation.* New York, McGraw-Hill, 1969.

---

11. *Ibid.,* p. 57.

SECTION VI
CONCERNS IN THERAPEUTIC RECREATION

International Symbol of Wheelchair Accessibility.

Courtesy of the Massachusetts Association of Paraplegics, Inc.

Photos taken at Northeastern University Easter Seal Unit at Camp Warren. Courtesy of Easter Seal Society for Crippled Children and Adults of Massachusetts, Inc.

CHAPTER 14

UNDERSTANDING THE USE OF PHARMACEUTICALS

Wes Arens

THE TOPIC OF DRUGS comes up in conversation and immediately there is an extra level of interest. Few of us go through life untouched by the action of drugs. In the field of therapeutic recreation many of the patients we deal with are taking pills for a multitude of reasons, varying from specific agents that directly aid in rehabilitating patients to the area of tranquilizers that act as support while the patient is learning to better cope with his handicap.

The intent of this article is simple—to communicate information about drugs to the recreational therapist in such a way that he will gain a better understanding of the pharmacotherapeutic needs of his patients.

Use and Application

A drug is any substance used as a medicine. The art of applying drugs in disease is termed "therapeutics." Although pharmacology is a branch of biology, its greatest interest lies in its relation to the treatment of disease. When the mode of action of a drug is understood, much greater accuracy can be obtained in the treatment. The object of pharmacology is to provide a scientific foundation for therapeutics and to increase the resources of the art of healing. Pharmacotherapeutics is the study of the use of drugs in the treatment of disease. The drugs used can be divided into two main classes pharmacodynamic and chemotherapeutic. The former type are used for their specific actions on the patient. They stimulate or depress physiological or biochemical functions in a way so predictable that they can be employed to alter the course of disease. Other drugs are administered to the patient for the purpose of destroying or inhibiting the growth of parasites. These are known as chemotherapeutic agents.

Mechanism of Drug Action

One of the most interesting and difficult fields of pharmacological research is that which deals with the mechanism of drug action. The action of drugs is variable but there are certain broad principles. These are stimulation, depression and irritation. Drugs which increase the activity of an organ or its function are said to stimulate it, while those which lessen the activity are said to depress it. Although the term irritation is often used as a synonym for stimulation, the conditions are not identical. Stimulation means an increase in the specialized function of a cell; irritation implies an action that produces slight temporary damage to tissues. Marked irritation can produce inflammation and death of tissue. An example of stimulation is caffeine which increases the activity of cells in the central nervous system. An example of irritation is castor oil which irritates the mucosa of the intestine and is said to act as a chemical irritant. When stimulation is prolonged or excessive, the tissue generally becomes depressed and finally loses its activity entirely. This is known as paralysis. Depression, whether induced directly or following stimulation, often resembles the fatigue induced by the prolonged exercise of the normal organ. When the effects of the drug are only temporary and the tissue returns to its normal activity, the drug is eliminated and the action is said to be reversible. When the cells do not recover, but have to be replaced by new growth, the action is irreversible.

On the sites of drug action, certain drugs act directly on effector cells. Others exert their action in a round-about manner. In some instances, the exact site of action is unknown. Drugs which act directly have two possible sites of action, the surface or the interior of the cell. Drugs which act in an indirect manner may exert their effects by promoting or preventing the action of another substance. An example of this would be many drugs used in the skeletal muscle relaxant field.

The characteristic action of a drug is intimately related to its chemical structure. There are many instances in which drugs of totally different chemical structure possess similar actions, especially those of the central nervous system depressants. Other drugs will alter their activity if the molecule is only slightly changed. An example of this would be in the development of antihistamines to reduce their soporific effect.

Drug Intake and Absorption

In the absorption of drugs, the absorption itself influences the choice of the route by which a drug is administered. The rate at which a therapeutic agent gains access to the circulation largely determines the period of giving the drug, the onset of action, and the intensity of action. The speed of absorption is also a factor in determining dosage. Of all factors which influence the absorption of drugs, the route of administration is the most important. Often there is a choice in the route of administration and the advantages and disadvantages of each different route is important. Drugs given orally are absorbed by the intestinal mucosa, and this is the oldest method of drug administration. Usually absorption is almost complete by the time the colon is reached. The advantages of oral administration are safety, convenience, and economy. The disadvantages are vomiting, drug destruction through the digestive action of body juices before they can be absorbed, and the predictability of response. Intestinal absorption may be irregular because of the influences of other substances in the G.I. tract, variation in emptying time of the stomach, or variation in the acidity of the intestinal contents. For example, some antacids interfere with absorption of some antibiotics, and taking mineral oil can block the absorption of vitamins.

The injection of drugs in the veins has certain advantages over oral administration which are of distinct value at times. It is essential when a drug must be absorbed in an active form. When time is urgent—for example, an emergency situation such as an anaphylactic shock—it can become of extreme importance. The disadvantages of the injection route could be the difficulty of self-injection by a patient, loss of patient control by a physician, and expense.

There are numerous methods of injection which I shall list

briefly. Subcutaneous—a shallow injection just beneath the skin which leads to a slow and even rate of absorption. Intramuscular —an injection deep into muscle tissue which also usually leads to a slow and even rate of absorption. This method, however, is not as slow or predictable as when given subcutaneously. Intraperitoneal—an injection into the peritoneal cavity used in laboratory procedures primarily. Intravenous—drugs are introduced in an isotonic solution directly into the vein. This offers immediate blood levels not possible by any other injection procedures, and therefore is used in emergency situations. Bone marrow—mainly used as an alternative route when intravenous infusions are impossible to give because of circulatory collapse, edema, extensive burns or thrombosis. Intrathecal—injection directly into the subarachnoid space used in spinal anesthesia.

Another route of administration is by inhalation. This method affords very rapid access to the blood stream. Solutions and suspensions of drugs can be atomized and the fine droplets or dry micronized particles inhaled. An example of this would be bronchodilating agents in the treatment of asthma.

Absorption of drugs also takes place readily through many of the mucous membranes in the body other than that of the alimentary canal. The sublingual, or under-the-tongue route of administration, permits rapid absorption of a variety of drugs. An example of this would be nitroglycerine used in the treatment of angina pectoris. A few drugs can penetrate the intact skin. Drugs introduced via the skin initiate an effect only on tissues in close proximity to the skin.

The absorption of a drug is dependent upon drug solubility. There are certain compounds which are so insoluble and chemically unreactive that they cannot be absorbed. The physical state of a drug also affects the rate of absorption. For example, a drug is more readily absorbed when given in solution, than when administered as a tablet. In this regard it is understandable that a drug will be absorbed into the body faster if its area of concentration is widened. The vascularity of the site from which a drug is being absorbed is a major factor influencing its rate as does its ability to circulate in the blood stream.

Drugs as a rule are distributed generally throughout the body in the medium of the body fluids. Certain agents, however, show definite affinities for particular tissues and accumulate there in high concentration.

Detoxification and Excretion

Drugs are detoxified or inactivated in the body by a variety of mechanisms. Many are oxidized, some are hydrolyzed, others are joined with chemicals in the body which tend to make them inactive. It is important to know in what organ a drug is detoxified; because, if there is an impairment of function in an organ, the giving of a drug may result in complications if the drug remains in its active form too long.

Each drug is excreted in a characteristic manner. It is often important to know the route and rate of excretion of a drug. Certain agents are removed from the body by a single channel. Others are eliminated by a number of routes. A drug is excreted unchanged or in the form of some breakdown product. The most important organs for the excretion of drugs are the kidneys, colon, and lungs.

Therapeutic Dosage

The dose of a drug greatly influences its action. Somewhere between the maximal and minimal dose of a drug lies the therapeutic dose. This therapeutic dose is influenced by many factors which must be considered when a drug is prescribed. These factors are age (as a rule children are more sensitive to drugs than are adults), body weight, sex (women are more susceptible to the actions of certain compounds than are men), time of administration (an amount of drug which is active before, may be ineffective if given after a meal; on the other hand, it may be tolerated if food is in the stomach in the case of irritating drugs), route of administration, and rate of excretion (important when chronic medication is required, because if a drug is repeatedly given and absorbed at a rate more rapid than it can be destroyed or excreted, then the concentration in the body will rise and toxic symptoms can occur). Drug combinations and tolerance of the person are also important factors.

Drugs often have side effects which doctors have learned to expect. Idiosyncrasy is an unusual response by a patient to a drug. Hypersensitivity is an allergic reaction to a given drug which can become a very serious problem. It may take many different forms such as skin reactions ranging from a mild rash to a severe dermatitis.

The physician's many years in training have disciplined his thinking about drugs and their use and abuse. His first concern to patients is to do no harm. Frequently, there are drug effects that his patient does not communicate to him. These are often picked up instead by his paramedical support team, including the recreational therapist. It is important for a recreational therapist to be aware of drug information, so he might better understand the reactions and mood of his patient as well as any limitations which ongoing drug treatment may impose. With knowledge of how drugs affect the patient, and when, the therapist can gear his program to better meet the recreation and therapeutic needs of each individual.

BIBLIOGRAPHY

American Journal of Nursing. New York, American Journal of Nursing Co.
Baker, C. E.: *Physicians' Desk Reference.* Oradell, N.J., Litton Pub., Inc., 1972.
Bergersen and Krug: *Pharmacology in Nursing.* St. Louis, Mosby, 1966.
Geriatrics. Minneapolis, Lancet Publications.
Goodman, L. S. and Gilman, A.: *The Pharmacological Basis of Therapeutics,* 3rd ed. New York, Macmillan, 1965.
Medical Letters, New York, Drug and Therapeutic Information, Inc.
The Merck Manual. Rahway, N.J., Merck Sharp and Dohme Research Laboratories.
Modell, W.: *Drugs of Choice.* St. Louis, Mosby, 1973.
Rational Drug Therapy, Bulletin of the American Society for Pharmacology and Experimental Therapeutics, Philadelphia, W. B. Saunders Co., Vol. 6, No. 1, Jan. 1972.

CHAPTER 15

IDENTITY PROBLEMS IN A HOSPITAL SETTING

Susan Mattes

Role identification in a hospital setting is still an on-going process for many therapeutic recreators. In some environments therapeutic recreation is understood and valued, usually after staff members have spent much energy coordinating professional relationships. More often, however, recreation therapy has little precedent on which to base its operation, and its uniqueness from the other health-care professions (i.e., nursing and the other therapies) makes it difficult to establish a place in the hospital. This struggle for acceptance requires therapeutic recreators to define the role, the method of operation and the specific values of their profession in a concrete way.

Role of the Therapeutic Recreator

Of these three aspects, role definition is probably the most difficult with which to deal. The confusion in deciding exactly what a recreation therapist is, or does, is often due to the fact that his function varies widely and is contingent upon the nature of individual institutions and their populations. This confusion is further complicated by the conflicting expectations held by others. For instance, the recreation therapist's job is to make judgments and initiate programs that will facilitate patient improvement. Medical personnel may ask whether the recreator has the knowledge to make these judgments competently since his education is not medically oriented; the implication being that ignorance is potentially harmful and may interfere with proper patient care. Here is raised the issue of exactly what constitutes a good degree program in therapeutic recreation. That is, what kind of preparation does a recreator need to operate effectively in a health-care environment? Further, do different facilities require varying kinds of preparation, i.e. rehabilitation facility vs. a mental health institution, children vs. adults, and so on? In visiting various facilities throughout Boston, authorities working with specific patient populations stress the importance of the recreator having extensive background in the field associated with the particular problem. A rehabilitation hospital director feels knowledge of anatomy and physiology to be essential, a mental health authority stresses psychology, and a children's hospital department head urges understanding of child development and learning disabilities. Does the therapeutic recreator really need such specialization in order to work professionally? Experience suggests, "no." Anyone who has worked in the field soon realizes that recreation takes countless forms, is readily adaptable to whatever handicaps and disabilities exist, and is worthwhile and beneficial in many ways. However, to those outside the field this conviction is not so strong. Thus, it is important for the recreator to undertake the responsibility of teaching the value of goal-oriented play to a work-oriented society.

This educative process must also direct itself at dispelling the notion of the recreator as a "babysitter," or someone to call on when a patient is bothersome and needs to be "kept busy." On the other hand is the view that it is the recreator, not the patient, who is truly bothersome, for recreation agitates, enlivens, and hopefully encourages assertive rather than passive patient response. Such responses are not always welcome; a passive status quo being more desirable and causing less interference with the "business of the hospital."

And finally, there are the patient expectations of the therapeutic recreator, of which there are two basic aspects. Some patients see the recreator as a person who tries to heal the spirit, a concerned party very much apart from doctors, nurses, and therapists, whose treatments must often cause physical discomfort. Other typically withdrawn patients greatly resist attempts to involve them with people and/or activities, either resenting the intrusion or being too depressed to willingly participate.

In the midst of all these inaccurate opinions about the purpose and function of recreation, the recreation therapist must perform his job. Here the identity problem is further complicated for the hospital recreator functions in a way totally unlike any other hospital staff member.

Method of Operation of the Recreation Therapist

The recreator works, of necessity, in what appears to be a very haphazard fashion. For instance, individual patient sessions or specific programs can be scheduled in only a limited way, working around the other therapies and hospital "goings-on." Therefore, the recreator must be prepared to take advantage of and use purposefully random moments when patient interest and free time coincide. Often the biggest obstacle is the patient himself. The recreator must be skilled in communicating with and motivating even the most withdrawn and resistant patients. The relaxed patient-recreator relationship that usually develops during sessions encourages close communication, making it necessary to keep sensitive as to what information should be imparted to the social worker, nurse or psychiatrist. These demands are essential and must be met, but not at the expense of diminished knowledge of or importance placed on the recreational program itself, for it is in the learning and doing of such skills and activities that health is promoted. Thus, the recreation therapist must be an expert teacher, able to instruct easily and to assess individual capabilities so that the recreational experience is always supportive and encouraging.

Value of Recreation in a Hospital Setting

It is the potential to give support and encouragement that makes recreation so valuable in a hospital setting. In fact, recreation therapy is one part of the slow but growing attempt by health care personnel to treat the person, not just the disease, and as a therapeutic resource, it is unique in several ways. For instance, people become "patients" when they are hospitalized, and thus are under the medical mandate that they are "sick." However, many in the recovery stages are more well than sick. The mandate then becomes incorrect and is a potential psychological barrier to early and complete recovery. Here, recreational participation is an excellent resource, providing a means for the patient to develop a self-image based on skill, independence, and social involvement, overcoming the tendency to cling to an identification with illness, isolation, and dependency. Also, recreational activities are as varied as patient needs, interests and abilities, and participation can be on an individual, small group, or large group basis. Thus, staff and policy permitting, all patients can be reached in some form or another. Lastly, recreation fills a multitude of needs at once by promoting socialization, heightening self-satisfaction, lessening and alleviating depression, and serving as an outlet for feelings of loss, anxiety and frustration. All of these needs and feelings are especially acute to a hospitalized population and a truly effective therapeutic recreation program will keep them in mind.

CHAPTER 16

TRENDS IN MUNICIPAL RECREATION SERVICES FOR HANDICAPPED PEOPLE

Debra S. Bloom

Introduction

FOR A NUMBER OF YEARS community recreators have been interested in the provision of services to handicapped children and adults. An increasing number of these programs are coming into existence. The Recreation Center for the Handicapped in San Francisco was established over twenty years ago. In 1955 the Community Council of Greater New York began a three-year demonstration project to show that handicapped children can have their recreational needs successfully met through existing community facilities.[1] One of the earliest articles to appear on the integration of the handicapped was in *Recreation* magazine in June of 1955 and was entitled "Boys and Girls Together—Handicapped and Ablebodied."[2] The City of Quincy, Massachusetts initiated its day camp for retarded children in 1956.[3]

In approaching the problem of providing municipal recreation services for handicapped persons we can follow the vocational rehabilitation model of three levels of service. The first level is that of an enabling service in which the recreation department would offer counseling to the "able-disabled" who, with very few adaptions, can fit into the regular on-going programs of the de-

---

1. Community Council of Greater New York, *A Report on Demonstration Project, Group Work with Handicapped Children*. New York, Community Council of Greater New York, 1959.

2. Herzog, John D.: Boys and girls together—handicapped and able-bodied. *Recreation*, 48:260-261, 1955.

3. William F. Ryan, Observation of a community recreation director on recreation for the retarded. *Recreation in Treatment, Centers*. Washington, D. C., American Recreation Society, 1964, Vol. III, pp. 16-17.

partment. This includes the majority of handicapped individuals. The second level is that of transitional service which would include recreation counseling, training in physical and social skills and providing the regular recreation staff with any information they might need to adapt their program materials to the special participant. Erickson cites a program of this type that Art Rubin used to help homebound multiple sclerosis patients acquire sufficient fishing skills to be able to participate in a citywide fishing derby.[4] The third level is the sheltered level for those whose handicap is so severe that there is little realistic likelihood of their being able to be integrated into many regular recreation programs. We see examples of this type of service in the program conducted at the National Recreation Association headquarters in New York in the early 1960's and the programs conducted at the Recreation Center for the Handicapped in San Francisco as well as the ANCHOR program in Hempstead, Long Island.[5] The majority of recreation services currently available to handicapped people probably fall into the second area. An earlier survey by the author of an eleven-town area of Massachusetts showed no Type I programs being offered. It is likely that the largest number of Type III programs, where they exist, are under the auspices of organizations other than municipal recreation departments, although they may make use of community recreation facilities.

Survey Information

An informal survey of 44 New England municipal recreation departments conducted in the spring of 1973 indicated that 75 percent of them currently offer some services to handicapped individuals. This is very interesting when compared with Hayes' 50 percent figure for Texas and Erickson's citing Andres' 55 percent figure.[6, 7] This can be viewed as growth in the number of

4. Eric Erickson, Meeting the recreational needs of special populations in the community. In Stein and Sessons (Eds.): *Recreation and Special Populations,* Boston, Holbrook Press, 1973, p. 51.

5. Morton Thompson, ANCHOR: A community recreation program for handicapped children. *Ther Rec J,* 6 (4) :167-171, 1972.

6. Gene A. Hayes and Dick Smith, Municipal recreation services for special populations in Texas. *Ther Rec J,* 7 (1) :28, 1973.

7. Erickson, *op. cit.,* p. 45.

services offered. All but one of the programs served retarded people. The majority of communities which work with both the mentally retarded and the physically handicapped included at least two and a half times as many mentally retarded people in their programs as physically handicapped. The number of individuals being served varied from one to 400 with the most frequent numbers being 25 to 50 retarded persons and from 5 to 30 physically handicapped persons. It might be noted that several of the municipalities responding did not give figures for the number of handicapped individuals served. Considering that an estimated 3 percent of the population is mentally retarded, the number being reached is very small. Even Boston and Worcester which have large special programs reach less than one-tenth of their handicapped populations. Table I shows the populations served in towns of varying sizes.

In addition to the physically handicapped and the mentally retarded, four communities provide programs for the emotionally disturbed and one offers a swimming program for learning disabled children.

Nineteen communities provided year-round programming, thirteen summer only, and one offered services only in the winter. Of those who have programs year-round, the majority place emphasis on their summer program for children, many of which are

TABLE I

RESPONDENTS GROUPED ACCORDING TO POPULATION AND THE PROVISION OF SERVICES TO VARIOUS SPECIAL POPULATIONS

Population	Total No. of Respondents	No. of Respondents Serving Special Groups	P.H.	M.R.	E.D.	L.D.
Under 9,999	9	2	1	2	0	0
10,000-19,999	8	7	3	5	1	0
20,000-29,999	8	6*	3	6	0	0
30,000-49,999	5	5	2	5	1	0
50,000-99,999	9	8	3	8	0	0
Over 100,000	5	5	3	5	2	1
Totals	44	33*	15	31	4	1

* One town is beginning a program this year but indicates there are handicapped persons integrated into its regular programs.

in the form of a day camp. Sixteen respondents indicated the inclusion of handicapped adults in their regular and/or special programs. Eighteen were aware of handicapped persons who are integrated into their regular programs and eight are unsure of the presence of handicapped people in their regular programs. This last datum may indicate true integration.

Below is a listing of the types of facilities used for the foregoing programs.

TABLE II

TYPES OF FACILITIES USED BY MUNICIPAL RECREATION DEPARTMENTS IN PROVIDING ACTIVITIES TO SPECIAL POPULATIONS

Schools and universities	14	Church	2
Parks	9	Bus	1
Camp	6	Recreation hall	1
Pool	6	YWCA	1
Community center	6	Bowling alley	1
Playground	4	Golf range	1
Gymnasium	4	Anything we can use!	1
Lake	2		

The variety of facilities in use supports the proposition that the elimination of architectural barriers makes public facilities available to all citizens. A supervisor in one community which provides only summer programs for its physically handicapped participants stated that this is due to the layout of the indoor winter facility which is inaccessible to people with physical limitations.

One of the first questions that arises in the development and provision of recreation programs for handicapped people is that of transportation. Hayes and Smith were surprised to find in their study of therapeutic recreation services offered by Texas municipalities that less than 80 percent of the respondents indicated transportation to be a problem.[8] The New England recreation departments handle transportation in a variety of ways with the largest number, twenty, using busses. Nine used taxicabs and eight leave the responsibility of transportation to the participants' family. Three use vans that belong to the recreation department, two said they use private cars and one uses Red Cross

---

8. Hayes and Smith, *op. cit.*, p. 27.

vehicles. Three more indicated that they provide transportation but did not specify the type. Janet Pomeroy takes the position that an adequate community recreation program for the handicapped should have its own busses and drivers.[9] Busses can be donated but gas, maintenance and drivers' salaries should be considered an essential part of the program from its inception. She points out that mini-busses are the most effective type to use. The Community Council of Greater New York Study indicated that money for special facilities would be better spent to transport clients to existing community programs and thereby serve more individuals.[10]

All the programs have paid staff. All but two augment the paid staff with volunteers. Of those responding to the question on staff-volunteer participant ratios, fourteen departments had more volunteers than staff. Eight used more staff than volunteers. Three apparently had equal numbers of staff and volunteers. Two communities had more volunteers than participants! Although certain programs use a 1:1 ratio of ablebodied persons to disabled, the most frequent ratio of those responding appeared to be 1:4.

Nearly one-half of those in the survey of Hayes and Smith wanted more information about handicapping conditions.[11] Nearly 40 percent would have liked more professionally trained staff. Pomeroy in her writings stresses that staff needs a strong recreation background and the flexibility to adapt to the special needs and abilities of disabled participants. According to Lunan, the camp at Little Grassy evolved at a time when little was known about recreational activities for the mentally retarded and the physically handicapped.[12] As a result, the counselors who had a strong skills background assumed no limitations on the part of

---

9. Janet Pomeroy, The role of municipal recreation departments in service to the mentally retarded individual. In Neal, Larry (Ed.) : *Recreation's Role in the Rehabilitation of the Mentally Retarded*, Eugene, Oregon, University of Oregon, 1970, p. 24.

10. Community Council of Greater New York, *op. cit.*, p. 25.

11. Hayes and Smith, *op. cit.*, p. 27.

12. Lunan, Bert, Little Grassy offers fun for handicapped campers. *Rehab Rec*, 9 (1) :23-25, 1968.

the campers and were able to develop an extensive and varied program.

Hayes and Smith expressed concern with the isolation in which programs for the handicapped are conducted and with the lack of correlation between the activities that are available in the institutions as compared with those offered to handicapped persons in the community setting.[13] Some institutional programs do utilize community programs and facilities as an integral part of therapeutic recreation services for patients.

Recreation departments cosponsor activity programs with other groups at the following rates: local school departments—17; local Associations for Retarded Children—14; Easter Seals—5; State Department of Education—3; and 1 each of other cosponsoring entities including civic organizations and two with the local mental health centers. It might be noted that in Massachusetts communities that sponsor recreation programs for physically handicapped and mentally retarded people are eligible for 50 percent expenditure reimbursement from the Special Education division of the State Department of Education. In 1971 91 Massachusetts municipalities made use of this funding source.[14] Although 31 of the respondents serve mentally retarded children and adults, it appears that only half the programs are cosponsored with local Associations for Retarded Children.

Program Offerings

The departments surveyed in this paper placed the emphasis on *recreation* and include fairly standard activities in their programs. No mention was made of wheelchair sports or square dancing. These have been in existence for many years and are spotlighted annually in the National Wheelchair Games on Long Island. The National Wheelchair Basketball Association has been in existence for more than a quarter of a century. Much of what

---

13. Hayes and Smith, *op. cit.*, p. 30.
14. Richard J. Pedro, *1971 Recreational Programs for Physically Handicapped and Mentally Retarded Persons.* Boston, Massachusetts Department of Education, n.d.

TABLE III

TYPES OF ACTIVITIES INCLUDED IN MUNICIPAL RECREATION PROGRAMS FOR SPECIAL POPULATIONS

Swimming	14	Music	2
Arts and crafts	10	Boating	1
Trips	8	Boy Scouts	1
Physical fitness	7	Cultural activities	1
Sports*	6	Drama	1
"Active and passive recreation"	5	Gym	1
"All recreation activities"	5	Slimnastics	1
Environmental awareness	3	Social	1
Bowling	2	Special events	1
Dancing	2	Special interest	1
Special playground	2	Special olympics	1

* Includes bocce, cricket, floor hockey, gymnastics and sailing.

is done in wheelchair sports occurs through self-help groups such as the National Wheelchair Athletic Association. Florescu published a guide for organizing wheelchair sports in any community.[15]

The most frequently offered activity was swimming. Several respondents stress that they offer *all* recreation activities to their special groups.

Since the question of activities was posed as an open-ended one rather than as a checklist it can be assumed that the named activities in Table III are representative of what is offered instead of being a comprehensive survey of what is available. Indicative of this point is that only one person mentioned Special Olympics when it is known to be an important facet of many New England recreation programs for retarded children.

In looking around the country to see some of the possibilities in special programming we find the Recreation Center for the Handicapped in San Francisco runs a special program for severely handicapped and retarded teenagers. This five-day-a-week program includes trips to the zoo, neighborhood walks, learning to use public transportation, homemaking skills, health education

---

15. Stefan Florescu, *Organizing Wheelchair Sports Events in Your City*. Lincoln Park, Mich., Stefan Florescu, 1968.

and grooming, literacy, developing hobbies that can be enjoyed at home, physical fitness, cultural activities, drama and theater, service projects, group trips and sex education classes. They also have a "workreation" program to prepare the mentally retarded for possible employment in programs in the community such as helpers for homebound recreation.[16] Buttonwood Farms in Pennsylvania has had a similar workreation program.[17]

Washington, D. C., has included language therapy in its program for the handicapped.[18] The recreation department in Seattle, Washington, has cooperated with a community mental health program in providing an overnight camping experience for former state hospital patients.[19] In Detroit a cooperative effort among the recreation department, the school department, the county Tuberculosis and Health Association and several hospitals produced a ten-week physical conditioning program for children with respiratory handicaps.[20]

Two programs which were not conducted in a community recreation setting, but could be, are weight training and winter camping. Weight training exercises for elementary school-aged retarded children were developed using cloth animals stuffed with seven, ten or fifteen pounds of buckshot.[21] The animals were more interesting to the children than conventional weights and provided greater motivation. A winter day camping program for retarded residents of the Brainerd, Minnesota State Hospital was begun in 1968 on a 140 acre site.[22] The program includes out-

---

16. Recreation Center for the Handicapped, Teen programs for the severely handicapped and retarded fact sheet. Jan., 1972.

17. Lester Mann and Martin Nayowith, Their hands are made for helping. *The Best of Challenge.* Washington, D. C., AAHPER, 1971, pp. 110-111.

18. *Ibid,* p. 199.

19. Charles Dunham, Community recreation for the psychiatric rehabilitant. *Ther Rec J* 5(3):113-116, 1971.

20. Herbert Hayden, Addie W. Suggs and Hilda Beaty, B is for breathing. *The Best of Challenge.* Washington, D. C., AAHPER, 1971, pp. 81-82.

21. James Lounsberry, Weight training for the mentally retarded at the primary level. *The Best of Challenge.* Washington, D. C., AAHPER, 1971, pp. 85-88.

22. Dick Endres, Winter camping with the mentally retarded at Camp Confidence. *J Health, Phys Educ Rec,* 43:86, 1972.

door cooking, tobogganing, ice skating, snow-shoeing, skiing, animal tracking and snowman building.

Other innovative programs that have been tried are modern dance and ballet for retarded children, exercises with a parachute for senior citizens and retarded children, an outdoor education facility constructed by retarded students, practice in voting for retarded adults, horseback riding and a family weekend at a motel for physically handicapped people and their families.

In a suburban area near Boston an effort is being made to develop a regional program of recreation for the handicapped. Several of the communities now offer small seasonal or year-round programs to school-aged handicapped youth, a number of whom already cross town lines to obtain recreation services. The precedent for regional programming in the area is regionalized cooperation in special education and a regional training workshop for summer recreation staff held last year. Interest in the program is being shown by recreation departments, special education staff, parent groups, handicapped adults, the state department of education and the state office of children's services. Among the benefits of a regional program are more efficient use of staff facilities, more economic transportation arrangements, a central resource point and the ability to provide more varied services.

Summary and Conclusions

The number of recreation departments offering services to handicapped persons is increasing. This is occurring primarily for the school-aged population. Many of the departments surveyed include some handicapped adults in their programs but none provide special adult groups for physically handicapped, mentally retarded or emotionally disturbed people nor is there anything for the homebound. With the nationwide trend toward deinstitutionalization of retarded persons and mental patients this is a serious lack. The trend toward normalization which is causing the elimination of special education classes in the schools may make it more difficult to reach individuals who could benefit from therapeutic recreation services in the community. With the method used in some localities of recruiting participants for recreation programs through the special education classes, only about half of the identified children enter the recreation programs. This can be a reflection of the fact that although public recreation is for everyone, not everyone has to use it. Methods need to be devised to insure ways of obtaining recreation for all who need and want leisure services.

Many departments have four season programming. With the exception of summer programs the majority of these are Saturday and/or one evening a week. There is room for increased year-round programming particularly for people who fall into the transitional and sheltered groups. These are the people who will have an overabundance of empty time in their lives if they lack leisure skills and opportunities.

The small numbers of physically handicapped people being served lends strength to the concept of regionalization. It can be seen that programs are now being offered with a minimum of special facilities and that transportation, although complicated and expensive, is being obtained.

Municipal recreators need to be careful to plan with and not just for the handicapped recipients of their services. There is a need to expand the programs to include opportunities for the participants to give service, particularly the adults. From the variety of programs discussed earlier in the paper it is evident that the program possibilities are limited only by the imagination of the staff and participants.

CHAPTER 17

ATTITUDINAL BARRIERS

Dwight Woodworth, Jr.

"Is anyone with you?" a deeply concerned woman asked a friend of mine not too long ago. Though my friend, out shopping with her five-year-old son, was taken aback by this question, incidents like this frequently occur for those in wheelchairs or with other noticeable disabilities. I'm sure this same questioner would never dream of making such an inquiry of a nondisabled person, so why should a disability make the difference? I certainly do not want to belittle gestures of humanity, but perhaps the reasons for such actions are rooted in the basic attitudes of the so-called "nondisabled" toward the disabled.

In his book, *Rehabilitation of the Physically Handicapped,* Henry Kessler concludes that the physically handicapped person ". . . bears a double burden, his actual disability and the social restrictions it incurs."[1] This implies that the disabled person, to be accepted in society, must overcome not only physical barriers such as stairs and narrow doorways, but also attitudinal barriers. Laws have been passed to attempt to alleviate the former, but what of the latter?

The question in my mind is just how far have we come in changing these attitudes? This was the subject of a pilot project I recently undertook. Though my study was conducted during a three-month period and is limited in scope, it perhaps indicates current attitudes toward the disabled.

Before exploring present attitudes, however, it might be profitable to look retrospectively at past attitudes of society toward the disabled. We find that in primitive societies, all those crippled and disabled were sacrificed for the good of the group.

---

1. Henry H. Kessler, *Rehabilitation of the Physically Handicapped,* New York, Columbia University Press, 1953, p. 19.

Such unwritten laws were furthermore carried over to the written laws of the ancients and determined the treatment of the disabled for many years. The Spartans, for example, left newborn infants who were suspected of being weak or defective to die of exposure. The Romans were perhaps a bit more humane in that they utilized the deformed as slave labor. This, of course, accounts only for those able to do physical labor, the helpless were conceivably disposed of. In medieval times deformity was associated with sin, the devil, and evil spirits, and a similar view was set forth by the doctrine of original sin in that a disability was considered punishment from God.

But we, the civilized, have come a long way from these ungrounded and detrimental beliefs—or have we? "There appears to be a basic American value that everyone should be equal," state Dibner and Dibner in a recent report.[2] At first this seems a noble value, but upon closer examination, we realize that this is a farce, and a harmful one at that. As Beatrice Wright noted: "It may be suggested that the concept of physical disability implies deviation from the normal standard, deviation from a state that is natural or average."[3]

Too often inequality and deviation from the norm connotes inferiority. Allow me to suggest that the disabled are sometimes looked down upon both literally and figuratively. Just as an adult looks down upon a young child, could it be that the standing nondisabled may unconsciously feel a sense of dominance or superiority over an individual in a wheelchair? This seems especially true in respect to the severely disabled with speech defects. They are often treated as young children unable to articulate and, as Jo Chapman points out: "Is there anyone who is severely disabled who has not been thought to be mentally retarded by someone who has just met him?"[4]

The feeling of inferiority is further emphasized in a 1968 re-

---

2. Andrew H. Dibner, Susan S. Dibner, *Integrated or Segregated Camping for the Physically Handicapped Child*, Easter Seal Society for Crippled Children and Adults, Mar. 1972, p. 21.

3. *Ibid.*, p. 21.

4. Jo Chapman, "The Changing Scene; Sexual Potential of the Handicapped." Metairie, Louisiana, Active Handicapped, May-June, 1970.

abled. Knowing the problems, he may be impatient for solutions. As for the student, I venture to hypothesize that perhaps he, along with other mildly disabled people, may reject the idea of associating with the disabled for fear that he will not be accepted by society. To my knowledge, there is no evidence other than my own experiences, to back this up, but I offer it as a point to ponder.

It is noteworthy to mention that the majority of the students indicated that they had personally known someone who was physically disabled, but this does not always result in differing attitudes. Research by William A. Anthony indicates that only information about a disability coupled with personal contact produces a significant attitudinal change.

In speaking of attitudes, whether social, educational, or vocational, one must always remember that it takes two to have a relationship. The attitudes of the disabled person are also important factors in his being accepted in society. This was pointed out to me in a letter from Frank G. Wood, Assistant Adjutant of the Disabled American Veterans. Wood states: "A recent study conducted by this office in conjunction with other business firms indicates that sometimes the veteran presents himself in a bad light. He seems to almost feel certain that because he is a disabled veteran, he is not going to get the job."

There are two major categories into which the disabled can be divided: those who are disabled at birth, and those disabled after birth. Indications are that those born with disabilities usually adjust better, although this is highly speculative, and since disabled veterans fall in the latter group, perhaps this is the reason for these negative feelings. In some instances, self-pity and bitterness result in the reaction to barriers, but I tend to think that the majority of disabled people are working to tear down these barriers.

Recent studies have been made to test the reactions of children to the disabled. In this area I asked respondents to complete the sentence, "Young children stare or fear those with physical disabilities because. . . ." M.A.P. members gave answers such as, "They see them as different," or "their parents have taught them to be quiet when they see one." Two more perceptive students felt that it was because they fear that they themselves will become disabled. This echoes the conclusion that Jason and Esser made after their three-year study of attitudes. They stated: "A physically normal person's aversion to the handicapped is fear of being struck by a similar fate."[6]

Dewey G. Force, Jr., in his article, "Social Status of Physically Handicapped Children," concluded that (1) many physically handicapped children are not accepted by their peers, (2) children with disabilities tend to associate with others having disabilities, and (3) children affected with cerebral palsy, the most visually obvious disability, were the least popular and those with heart conditions, the least visually obvious were accepted the most.[7] The third point, however, is contradicted by other studies indicating that nondisabled children sometimes reject the even mildly impaired because of their inability to keep up or play according to the rules of a particular game.

Another area I dealt with was that of personal relationships either between two disabled people or a disabled and a nondisabled. Are the disabled looked upon as ascetics with the myth of the Handicapped Saint surrounding them? I asked if individuals would consider dating a disabled person. Oddly enough, two from each group said they would not. Three of the M.A.P. members left this blank or indicated that "it depended."

Are physically disabled people sexually maladjusted? Five from the student group felt that they were, but then an equal number from the M.A.P. group also answered affirmatively. Should most marry? One student felt they should not marry and two M.A.P. members agreed. As for having children, either through conception or adoption, one student and one M.A.P. member agreed that disabled persons should not be parents. The curious thing was that the student who felt that the disabled should not marry indicated that most were capable of parenthood.

The disabled want to be accepted as full-fledged members of society, but just how will this come about? Who should make the

---

6. Hostility to the handicapped. *Time,* 96(25):67, 1971.

7. Dewey C. Force, Jr., Social status of physcially handicapped children. *J Excep Child,* 23:104-107, 1956.

first move? In reference to these questions, I asked what society should do. M.A.P. members stressed the need to educate the general public, to stress worth and ability—too often shadowed by disability—and to foster integration. There were both positive and negative responses from the student group. Some felt that society should "treat them as nondisabled or normal," and "accept them for what they are, not how they appear." Others responding more negatively, felt that society should "help them overcome their hang-ups." The most apathetic was simply "do nothing."

As previously stated, acceptance is a two-way street, so I next asked what the disabled should do to be accepted. M.A.P. members felt they should "be themselves and let society decide," "find opportunities to use (their) abilities," and "accept society and its flaws." More assertive answers were that they should "organize and work as one group to demand their rights as human beings" and not ". . . expect to be treated as anything but a member of society." The students felt that they should "overcome feelings of being different," "try harder than the nondisabled," and just "be themselves." I thought it unusual, however, that someone suggested that they "stay in the background."

The disabled will no longer stay behind closed doors, nor should they. All have abilities to contribute, and I think society is beginning to realize this. Attitudes and knowledge of them are important in the rehabilitation and habilitation processes of those with physical, mental and emotional disabilities. More research needs to be done in this area for, as the Massachusetts Vocational Planning Commission reports: "Unless more is known about the nature of attitudes and their formation . . . special educational techniques and methods to effect needed changes will be difficult to develop and apply."[8]

Perhaps the day draws near when society will see people, not as disabled individuals neatly pigeon-holed as a dependent group, but as distinct individuals who just happen to have noticeable disabilities.

---

8. *Helping All the Handicapped*, The report of the Massachusetts Rehabilitation Planning Committee, 1968, p. 173.

CHAPTER 18

ARCHITECTURAL BARRIERS

Nancy K. Williams

The Frustrations

To the average American born into an increasingly specialized technological/industrial society, many opportunities abound and many responsibilities are given. As the American draws from his country's offerings, so he is expected to "put back"; ideally in the same proportions. To live he must work; to work he must have received some education. Many challenges and demands are to be met before he can make his contribution. This is the rewarding process of a lifetime which poses only *special* problems to the *usual* person, but *usual* problems to the *special* person.

Who is the "special person"? Legally, he is:

> a person confined to a wheelchair, a person who, because of the use of braces or crutches or because of the loss of a foot or leg or because of an arthritic, spastic, pulmonary or cardiac condition, walks with difficulty or insecurity, a person who, due to a brain, spinal or peripheral nerve injury, suffers from a faulty coordination or palsy, a person who is blind or whose sight is so impaired that functioning in a public area, he is insecure or exposed to danger, a person whose hearing is so impaired that he is unable to hear warning signals, and a person whose mobility, flexibility, coordination and perceptiveness are significantly reduced by aging.[1]

Or, this refers to today's 5,000,000 people with heart irregularities, 250,000 in wheelchairs, 200,000 with heavy leg braces, 139,000 with artificial limbs and 18,000,000 men and women over 65 years of age.[2] Every year we add to the list. Dr. Howard A. Rusk has

---

1. The Commonwealth of Massachusetts, Department of Public Safety, *Rules and Regulations of the Board to Facilitate the Use of Public Buildings by the Physically Handicapped*, p. 3.
2. Easter Seal Society for Crippled Children and Adults of Philadelphia, Bucks, Chester, Delaware and Montgomery Counties, *Don't Build Architectural Barriers!*

stated that by 1980, for every ablebodied person in this country, there will be either one person with a physical disability, one person with a chronic illness, or one person over 65 years of age.[3]

And why are there difficulties confronting these impressive numbers of people? If structures are designed for our least able person would they not be accessible to all people? We know that severely impaired persons have distinguished themselves in such positions as President of the United States, governors, mayors, architects, poets, musicians, lawyers, businessmen, inventors, social workers, etc., but we also know that this is not the rule. Many disabled people have been thwarted in their attempts to achieve realistic life goals that were well within their potential. Aside from psychological barriers, it is the physical barriers that keep the physically handicapped people off our streets and outside our buildings. Since physical barriers to the handicapped are usually built into buildings by the thoughtlessness of architects, they have become known as "architectural barriers."[4]

Architectural barriers make it very difficult for the physically handicapped to project themselves into many normal situations. The most common design and construction of thousands of buildings and facilities such as schools, clinics, community centers, libraries, post offices and airports, many times do not accommodate the handicapped person and therefore limit, restrict, or otherwise interfere with his life style. As he watches, the simple routines of his daily affairs become quite complicated, if not impossible, and the handicapped person tends to lose hope and needlessly lower or abandon his goals. The greatness of the problem is appreciated when we realize that one out of every nine persons in the United States is denied free access to the building in which he may want to work, vote, worship, learn, play or even make a phone call because architectural barriers make it virtually impossible for him to enter.[5]

In a study conducted by the Massachusetts Association of Para-

---

3. Leon Chatelain, Jr., More accessibility for handicapped. *Rehab Rec,* Nov.-Dec., 1966, p. 12.

4. *Ibid.,* p. 1.

5. Robert Dantonia and Benjamin Tessler, Architectural barriers for the handicapped, a survey of the law in the United States. *Rehab Lit,* 28 (2) :35, 1967.

plegics, Incorporated, it was found that 81 percent of the handicapped citizens in the state are in the 21 to 59 age range and 49 percent of these are in wheelchairs. So let's take a young man of 25 years who is confined to a wheelchair and examine the architectural barriers he has faced from birth, presently faces and will continue to face in his quest to become a taxpayer and contributor to society rather than a tax responsibility.

Perhaps the first social institution known to a child is the public school. Many handicapped boys and girls who do not require special education services, have a choice of needlessly spending their time in special schools or receiving makeshift education at home because architectural barriers exclude them from attendance at the regular school. In the public school that has neglected the needs of the special child, barriers include heavy and cumbersome doors, slippery, narrow corridors, stairways and no elevators, inaccessible bathroom facilities, drinking fountains that are too high, desks that are too low and chalkboards that are unreachable. Consequently, as the M.A.P. study points out, 32 percent of the handicapped people in the Commonwealth do not graduate from high school.[6] These figures may not be particularly reflective of the problem as they do not make a distinction between children who have been in wheelchairs all their lives and ones who have had traumatic accidents or diseases which have put them in wheelchairs at a later age. The percentage would increase for those people who have been disabled before reaching school age.

The college-bound person in a wheelchair is obstructed in all these ways, and more. His selection of accessible colleges, although growing, is still meager. In many cases he will be barred from the college of his choice, and will have to settle for another on the basis of its total or partial accessibility. Typical barriers encountered on a college campus include all those found in the secondary school plus: lack of walkways without steps connecting the different buildings on campus, absence of seating arrangements in auditoriums (inaccessibility to theatrical entertain-

---

6. A study conducted by the Massachusetts Association of Paraplegics, Inc., "Housing needs of the handicapped," November 1970, p. 18 and 22.

ment, and class lectures) and parking facilities which are not usable. Thus, only 7 percent of the physically handicapped graduate from college; 6 percent post-graduate.[7]

As we have seen, architectural barriers unnecessarily interfere with education of those who most require educational opportunities to become self-sustaining. School buildings need not be completely remodelled to eliminate barriers. In many instances, relief may be offered at a nominal cost. This small additional cost is greatly offset by the fulfillment of personal potential and a contribution to society by persons who, although handicapped, become skillful, productive members of society.

Architectural barriers exist everywhere today, but in no place do they limit the handicapped from achieving his full potential more than in the home. Once on his own, if able, the handicapped person desires to be as independent as possible, and indeed, independence is only as possible as his housing facilities will allow. Newlyweds or single people who are looking at buildings will sight innumerable problems innate in all modern apartments. Most new apartments are wall-to-wall carpeted. This presents problems as carpeting catches in the wheels of a wheelchair and hinders movement; bathrooms and bedrooms are inaccessible and kitchens are often totally unusable as many modern ovens are wall ovens and most counters, cabinets and refrigerators exceed the distance reachable for someone in a wheelchair. Height of dining room tables is wrong, closet arrangements are impossible and, of course, the usual entrance and exit problems exist. Partly due to architectural barriers, 60 percent of people in wheelchairs need some form of assistance on a daily basis.[8] Housing, then, is a serious problem as very little of it is designed with the physical limitations of the handicapped in mind and that housing which is, or could be made usable is too expensive. Thus, it has been estimated that at least one-half of all handicapped people are living in housing which they consider to be inadequate.

Inability to function in their own homes also seems to extend

---
7. *Ibid.*, p. 19.
8. *Ibid.*, p. 27.

outward when the handicapped person desires to leave his home. Transportation problems (inability to get to and from) include inaccessibility to busses and subways. As with other architectural areas, it seems that transportation facilities also are designed with only 90 percent of the population in mind. Most handicapped people who cannot use or afford a specially equipped car, have only taxicabs as an alternative. This form of transportation is quite expensive; thus it has been found that the vast majority of wheelchair people seldom or never use taxi service, and thus, remain virtually immobile.[9]

It is approximated that 52 percent of the people in wheelchairs are unemployed at present.[10] This is so, no doubt, for a variety of reasons, but architectural barriers, as we have seen, strike out against the handicapped person's employment.

What is being done? National recognition of this problem got its start with the passage of the Vocational Rehabilitation Act of 1954. However, it wasn't until 1959 that actual standards were set up in a serious attempt to eliminate architectural barriers. These standards, developed under the sponsorship of the President's Committee on Employment of the Handicapped and the National Society for Crippled Children and Adults and with the assistance of the American Standards Association, are published: *American Standard Specifications for Making Buildings and Facilities Accessible to, and Usable by, the Physically Handicapped.*

On October 31, 1961, after a two-year study by the American Standards Association (A.S.A.), these building standards were fully approved and adopted. The standards would indeed solve the problem of architectural barriers, were they strictly adhered to; however, they aren't always followed. The state of South Carolina, on May 7, 1963 was the first to approve and adopt in full the standards set forth by the A.S.A. This set a precedent for other states as the Council of State Governments to Reduce Architectural Barriers drafted its legislation based upon the South Carolina Act of 1963. Since that time, over half of the states have risen to the challenge of accepting the standards, how-

---

9. *Ibid.,* p. 24.
10. *Ibid.,* p. 20.

ever some only in part. Many states include or have included "escape clauses" in their laws which render their enforcement ineffective and inadequate. Massachusetts, for instance, in 1962, included a Chapter 662 which stated that:

> ... all plans and specifications for the erection of public buildings by the Commonwealth or any political sub-division thereof shall provide facilities for the handicapped to the extent deemed feasible by the contracting authority . . . that insofar as feasible and financially reasonable in the opinion of said contracting authority said facilities shall conform with the booklet entitled *American Standard Specifications for Making Buildings and Facilities Accessible to, and Usable by, the Physically Handicapped*. . . .

However, the escape clause "deemed feasible" by the "contracting authority" was amended in 1967 with Chapter 724; an act:

> Establishing a Board to adopt rules and regulations for the construction and maintenance of public buildings for the purpose of facilitating the use of such buildings by physically handicapped persons.

This Board which is comprised of:

> . . . the commissioner, or a member of the department designated by him in a writing filed with the state secretary, the commissioner of administration, or his designee, and five members appointed by the governor. . . . At all times at least three of the appointive members of the board shall be physically handicapped persons. . . .

was to have:

> . . . all necessary powers to require compliance with its rules and regulations, and modifications thereof and substitutions therefor, including power to institute and prosecute proceedings in the superior court to compel such compliance. . . .

However, even with the addition of this act, actual enforcement was not happening and yet another act, Chapter 827, was drawn up and finally passed in 1971 which further defined the term "public building" to include:

> "privately financed buildings that are open to and used by the public" i.e. "transportation terminals, institutional buildings, commercial buildings exceeding two stories in height or employing more than forty persons, buildings having places of assembly or a capacity of more than one hundred and fifty persons, public areas in funeral

homes, rest rooms in shopping centers, hotels, motels and dormitories."

Thus, in effect, very little attention was paid between 1962 and 1971 to actual resolution; needs of the handicapped person were still being ignored. Even now, many inaccessible public buildings are going up because inspectors are not doing their jobs. They have the laws, but are not following them through. Presently Senate Bill #868, once unfavorably voted out, is up again to be voted upon. This Bill provides that an "inspector or inspectors of buildings shall enforce and inspect the rules and regulations adopted in accordance with the provisions" of everything that has been passed so far. Let's hope this works!

The Laughs

It is true, architectural barriers close many doors to the handicapped person. But every now and then we hear of those "special doors" that only open to a wheelchair. For instance:

Word has finally leaked out that a certain museum in town is holding back certain secrets from the public. Strangely enough, people in wheelchairs say they "don't mind one bit" entering the museum through its basement. It seems that this basement is the storage place for all material considered, if you'll excuse the expression, "erotic." Sources within wheelchair circles are saying: "it is quite the collection."

Of course most people in wheelchairs feel that they could be volunteer health inspectors as they see practically all the kitchens in town, on their way into restaurants. However, sometimes the wheelchair comes in very handy when a restaurant is real crowded and they won't accept reservations or let a chair through the kitchen. A young man once told me that he went to such a place in New York City with three other people. Before leaving home, they called the restaurant to check on entrances. "No problem" they were told "we'll just open up the side doors." When they arrived there was a very long waiting line outside but the host singled them out of the line, whizzed them over to the side door and let them right in. No wait. The other people in line could be heard saying, "Hey, no fair; where do I get one of those chairs?"

A restaurant may not always be aware of its own architectural barriers. My friend in the wheelchair was once told over the phone that a restaurant he wanted to eat in was accessible, and upon arrival he found that it was not. When this happens to a person in a wheelchair who has traveled a long distance to get there and is very, very hungry and there is no convenient restaurant nearby, he will usually demand to be taken inside. If this means, and it usually does, that he is carried in, wheelchair and all (that goes 255 lbs. in my friend's case) he figures he has scored three points:

> The people who carried him will not forget the next time someone else calls. The restaurant is made aware of its barriers and he meets his needs.

There is always the old drive around and around and around the restaurant technique to see if you can spy any accessible entrances on your own. Of course this may prove near fatal if a policeman gets the idea that you are sizing the place up to plant a bomb or something. My friend has been stopped before for suspicion.

Then there was the case of a girl in a wheelchair and her friend who, one rainy day, was wheeling around a particular restaurant they wanted to try, testing each entrance. They couldn't get the wheelchair through any of them. Finally the girl pushing the wheelchair got tired and left the girl in the wheelchair out front while she went inside to confer with the management about the problem. Meanwhile, the rain had stopped and the girl in the wheelchair took her rain hat off and set it in her lap, facing up. Suddenly, passers-by in the street began dropping coins in the hat. The girl tried to protest and explain "No, but I have a job," no one listened. Everyone smiled. By the time her friend got back, the girl had collected a sum of two dollars and fifty cents.

It is easy to rip-off movie theaters while you are in the wheelchair without really trying—it just happens. Either the person is given a flat "no, you cannot come in" or everyone goes completely out of his way, "hovering over" and generally creating such a big fuss that they completely forget to collect the tickets.

I am sure volumes could be written along these lines, but the laughs hardly compensate for the enduring daily frustrations encountered by the disabled.

BIBLIOGRAPHY

"American Standard Specifications for Making Building and Facilities Accessible to and Usable by, the Physically Handicapped." American Standards Association, New York, October 1961.

Chatelain, Leon, Jr.: More accessibility for handicapped. *Rehab Rec*, Nov.-Dec., 1966, pp. 11-25.

Dantona, Robert and Tessler, Benjamin: Architectural barriers for the handicapped: A survey of the law in the United States. *Rehab Lit*, 28(2):34-43, 1967.

Easter Seal for Crippled Children and Adults of Philadelphia, Bucks, Chester, Delaware and Montgomery Counties. *Don't Build Architectural Barriers!* Making facilities accessible to the physically handicapped. State University Construction Fund, Albany, New York, July, 1967.

The Illinois Commission for Handicapped Children: Architectural blocks in school buildings: The problem and the solution. March, 1954.

A Study Conducted by the Massachusetts Association of Paraplegics, Incorporated, in cooperation with the Massachusetts Council of Organizations of the Handicapped under contract from the Massachusetts Rehabilitation Commission: Housing needs of the handicapped. November, 1970.

CHAPTER 19

TOWARD INTEGRATION

Frank M. Robinson, Jr.

Introduction

WHEN WE DISCUSS the integration of disabled people into society we usually refer to those children and adults who are handicapped to a minimal or moderate degree. Seldom do we consider the severely disabled person or promote programs which have as one of their goals to socially integrate them with ablebodied individuals. Such a unique program has been the ongoing Massachusetts Easter Seal unit at Camp Henry Warren which is owned and operated by Northeastern University. Although this program has been in operation for the past three summers, concentration for this brief study is only on the all male 1972 season. The camp has since become coed. My purpose is to analyze the integration process and to determine and appraise those severely disabled boys who were most successful in social mixing.

The Setting

Northeastern University's Warren Center for Physical Education and Recreation is a year-round outdoor laboratory and conference center located in Ashland, Massachusetts on 120 acres of open fields, woodland and lakeside with excellent facilities for group living and program accommodations. During the summer months it is used primarily for camping, hence named Camp Warren. The camp houses simultaneously a resident program for inner-city boys administered by the Physical Education Department and a special unit financed by Easter Seals and administered by the Recreation Education Department.

A specially designed barrier-free cottage for severely disabled boys is located closest to the main lodge with similar housing facilities further down the path for the ablebodied campers. Faculty from the two departments direct each camp and coordinate the program, with trained and qualified students working as the counselors. Medical supervision, food service, maintenance and secretarial assistance complete the staff complement. The Easter Seal unit also utilizes dedicated teenage volunteers from the immediate and surrounding areas. During each session 75 ablebodied inner-city boys camp together with 15 severely disabled boys; a ratio of 5 to 1. This program is in keeping with the Massachusetts Easter Seal philosophy of providing services in cooperation with existing facilities and promoting integration whenever possible.

The two camping programs operate independently during daily activity periods coming together for meals, evening programs and special events. The youngster who leaves the physical education group to mix does so of his own choosing. Our low key approach is to cultivate meaningful relationships through education and by demonstrating that the disabled camper also has abilities. More importantly, that he is a human being and deserves to be treated the same as everyone else. During free time many inner city boys take an interest in our high-spirited counselors and the diversified activities they organize. This leads to a mingling of both camper groups and the development of social interaction and rapport. Although the division of programs does not necessarily foster and encourage the integration of people, it does, however, provide a model for integration which is more realistic of society in general. Under this structure if integration of people is to occur, the reasons will be more natural and humanistic than if these groups were forced upon one another. A natural outdoor environment stressing activity and fun, provides the ideal therapeutic community setting for integration to flourish.

The Mixture

The boys referred to the special unit are, in most instances, too severely disabled to attend a regular agency camp. Their problems are often multiple requiring a great amount of care and supervision. The large percentage of boys confined to wheelchairs frequently need help in dressing, toileting, lifting and feeding. Those who were ambulatory, with or without support, had complications including speech, vision, emotions, heart, blood vessels, retardation and others. Most of these boys were reared under the protection of a sheltered environment. Few of them ever experienced normal social relationships with peers during their developmental years. Many were socially isolated.

The non-handicapped economically deprived boy on the other hand, was a tough, self-sufficient and extremely active youngster. He had grown up having to fight his own battles and make his way independently. These inner-city boys had learned to respect physical strength and ability, the direct opposite of the disabled campers who portray physical weakness. What did these youngsters have in common or what could they do together? Would the difference be too great? Will the strong learn to accept and respect the severely disabled?

Analyzing the Disabled Campers

Although the Easter Seal unit at Camp Warren is designed for boys who are severely disabled, all of the campers do not fit into this category. One or two each session could be fully integrated into a regular agency camp which perhaps will happen another year. Having a few mildly disabled boys with capabilities lightens the counselors' load. They assist around the cottage and spearhead the movement toward integration.

Of the 55 different disabled boys who attended camp (some attended more than one session) 47 percent required wheelchairs all of the time; 14 percent used crutches or canes and 39 percent were ambulatory most of the time. The wheelchair percentage increased during the course of the summer as some heavily braced boys used a chair alternately with crutches. Approximately 77 percent of the boys either went to a special school for the disabled, attended a special class at a regular school, or had a home teacher. Only 23 percent were fully integrated in their schooling. A portion of this figure represents mentally alert boys in wheelchairs showing that some towns have made strong efforts toward integration. A large majority of the boys, 73 percent, still live at home while 27 percent reside in state institutions. The first three two-week sessions primarily served severely disabled boys within the normal intellectual range. The fourth session accommodated severely disabled boys who were also mentally retarded. Age range was basically seven years to twenty, with a few exceptions.

In determining the problem areas of care, communications and supervision, we consider it a problem only if the camper absolutely requires our help to perform a function despite encouragement to manage independently. For instance, if a boy needs only a guard to be secured around his plate by the counselor, but otherwise can feed himself, this camper is not considered as having a feeding problem. Likewise, a camper in diapers who has to be changed four or more times each day by the counselor, has a definite toileting problem but is counted only once. Although no attempt is made to measure the degree of care, this listing does, at least, indicate the problem areas and the number of campers having them. Typically, each child in a wheelchair will have three or four related problems which are counted separately below. It should also be noted that five boys, for all our intents and purposes, are considered entirely free of these problems. The remaining 50 campers have *one or more* of the following *problems requiring special care and supervision*

Feeding	8 campers
Toileting	22 campers
Dressing and self care	34 campers
Lifting	26 campers
Communications	24 campers
Supervision	32 campers
Other care	4 campers
	140

Distributing the 140 camper problems over the 55 disabled boys at camp during the summer averages 2.5 such problems per disabled camper. This criteria gives some indication of group severity.

Developing Potential

Perhaps the greatest challenge of the staff during each brief two-week session is to discover what each individual is able to do, to cultivate this potential and then to find a way that it can be expressed. The integration process and the human personality is enhanced when a skill, interest or ability is developed and recognized. Each individual needs to find his place to shine in the sun.

Our search to discover human potential begins the very first day, when the counselors talk informally with campers and parents on arrival. Prior to this we pick up clues from the camper application, school report and social worker's interview sheet. Each counselor during activities will note any special interest which can be developed. We strive to activate the slogan "it's ability, not disability, that counts." Sometimes we just happen to fall upon a special skill when a boy in a wheelchair shows a special technique in catching fish or a paraplegic exhibits skill at archery from his wheelchair. Frequently the investigation is a very difficult one, particularly if the camper has a multiple handicap. Examples are:

Boy confined to wheelchair with Freidreich's ataxia becomes fascinated with playing the kazoo and is soloist during group performance.

Camper who is mongoloid and can utter only the sound "baa" is featured in whiffenpoof song during special event.

Individual with brain damage, as a result of an accident, wins breath holding contest at the all-camp water carnival.

Boy who is quadriplegic cerebral palsied, with no speech, is supported by counselor while performing the perfect rendition of a hula dance to music at open house.

Blind camper who learns to play the drums is given the spotlight at talent show.

Boy with spina bifida, confined to wheelchair, is taught Indian wrestling and discovers that he can whip every ablebodied boy in camp.

The counselors and volunteers share information on campers and expose each one to a myriad of activities and experiences. The informal play and close relationships tend to release tension and help the camper reveal some of his inner wants or strengths. In two weeks, or maybe a lifetime, you cannot hope to conquer a child's problems, satisfy his needs or even teach him how to play a simple game. You can, however, with persistence, find a tiny spark of potential in everyone which can be set aflame with proper ventilation. This is our challenge.

Fostering Integration

Integration of children happens naturally, freely and very candidly. At first the ablebodied youngster will stare, then many will muster enough courage to ask questions. "Can't you walk? . . . Why do you have that bag? . . . Did you get in an accident or were you born that way?" Some pass the curiosity stage very fast and once the questions are answered and understood human relationships develop and the disabled youngster becomes accepted as a person. The approach may then be, "Can I push you to the dining hall? . . . Do you want to play hockey?" It is a delight to observe the severely handicapped and ablebodied boys playing together, talking together and laughing together as companions accepting each other despite obvious differences. Naturally only some of the disabled boys and nondisabled boys enjoyed social integration while others would never be seen mixing. It is to this point that I conducted an observational study, with the aid of counselor reports, to determine which campers integrated successfully and why. The following observations were made of the 55 disabled boys regarding their *play and associations:*

4—associated and preferably played with ablebodied boys
19—associated and played with both groups—no preference
21—preferred to play and associate with only the disabled group
11—required counselors or volunteers to initiate play.

As expected, the four boys who preferred to associate and play with the nonhandicapped were the most physically active and capable with no visible impairment. The one exception was a boy who is totally blind, but has a very high intellectual level. The 11 boys observed as needing counselor stimulation were among our most severely handicapped. Nine have no speech and the other two have emotional problems which impede socialization. From this criteria 23, or 42 percent of the disabled boys successfully integrated with the ablebodied campers.

A separate observation was made to determine which disabled

boys were liked by the nondisabled campers. This was gauged by cheers, applause at events or an expressed interest in the camper. It was also noticed in individual reactions of one toward the other. A willingness to speak or go out of the way just to say "Hi, Rusty," indicated some feeling of fondness or acceptance. The following criteria rates each disabled camper according to how he was perceived by the ablebodied in the areas of *popularity and acceptance:*

    4—most popular in camp, known and liked by all
    11—accepted and popular—both groups
    19—moderately accepted and popular—both groups
    17—accepted only by disabled group
    4—least accepted by disabled group.

Three of the four top ranking boys in this category are severely disabled in wheelchairs. One boy's primary disability is osteogenesis imperfecta. He is of dwarf size, severely deformed and yet his cheerful attitude, polite manner, infectious laugh and outgoing personality were outstanding characteristics. He was respectfully labeled the Mayor of Camp. Another boy was quadriplegic cerebral palsied with a radiant smile and a zest for life that was contagious. He lived to the hilt of his capacity despite the severity of his impairment which included lack of speech. He had a tendency to walk his wheelchair from a sitting position and everyone welcomed his friendly visits. The third boy was severely impaired with spina bifida. He is an actor, extremely personable, talkative and enthusiastic. His mannerisms were mimicked with affection. From his wheelchair he would lead the entire camp in song to the enjoyment of all. The fourth camper was a victim of an accident which left him hemiplegic, hyperactive, and confused. He was prone to run off, to pick up rocks and to invent any number of acts to challenge the counselors. Although sometimes deeply distressed, he was gifted with an amazing sense of humor and a personality which could lift the entire camp. He was loved by everyone.

  Of the four boys least accepted by even the disabled group, one had an odor problem with his catheter, one was emotionally insecure and frequently unsociable, another severely retarded and the fourth camper was clumsy, completely speechless, unable to relate to his cabinmates, and frequently detached from their play. From this criteria thirty-four, or approximately 62 percent of the disabled campers integrated to at least a moderate degree.

It is interesting to note that the four top rated disabled boys listed in each of these two criteria are different boys, thereby inferring that the ability to play and associate together has no relationship to popularity and acceptance, for social integrative purposes. This relationship could be further explored.

Programs which fostered integration more than others were the ones in which the disabled and ablebodied campers participated together; the ones in which they could learn from one another and gain a greater appreciation of the talents and human qualities of each. Such programs were the all-camp Olympic games, the water carnival, open house, skit night, casino night, the award and talent presentation as well as free time activity which fostered social interaction.

Conclusions

In sum, it can be noted from this informal observational study that, whereas only 23 percent of the severely disabled boys were integrated at school, 42 percent (associated and played) to 62 percent (accepted and popular) of their total number integrated sufficiently at camp. Also, while 27 percent of the campers reside in state institutions, a segregated facility, 33 percent of this group (associated and played) to 66 percent (accepted and popular) integrated with the ablebodied boys at camp.

The notion that two severely impaired institutionalized boys were judged to be among the most popular and accepted campers may be hard to believe in some quarters. This either speaks favorably for the work of some of our state institutions or indicates that the boys should not have been there in the first place.

This brief study strongly dispells any beliefs that severity of disability, age, place of residence or educational background affects integration in a camping situation. It is also apparent that personality plays the major role in acceptability, and it is on this development that integration hinges. The disabled individual with a friendly, socially attractive personality can integrate readily at camp. If he can also contribute something to the group, his chances of success will increase. It is conceivable that disabled individuals who successfully mix at camp will make a satisfactory social adjustment to school and to the community. It is also conceivable that if two of our more diverse groups, the economically deprived and severely handicapped, can get along favorably and move significantly toward integration our larger society should be able to do the same.

I don't know what your
destiny will be,
but one thing I know:
    The ones among you
      who will really be happy
are those
who have sought and found
    how to serve

          ALBERT SCHWEITZER